# ECONOMIC GROWTH
# AND TRANSITION

Econometric Analysis of Lim's S-Curve Hypothesis

# Economic Growth Centre Research Monograph Series

Series Editor:  Euston Quah                    **ISSN:**
                *(Nanyang Technological University, Singapore)*

Vol. 1   Economic Growth and Transition: Econometric Analysis of
         Lim's S-Curve Hypothesis
         by Hui Ying Sng *(Nanyang Technological University, Singapore)*

Economic Growth Centre Research Monograph Series – Vol. 1

# ECONOMIC GROWTH AND TRANSITION

## Econometric Analysis of Lim's S-Curve Hypothesis

### Sng Hui Ying

Nanyang Technological University, Singapore

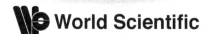

**World Scientific**

NEW JERSEY · LONDON · SINGAPORE · BEIJING · SHANGHAI · HONG KONG · TAIPEI · CHENNAI

*Published by*

World Scientific Publishing Co. Pte. Ltd.

5 Toh Tuck Link, Singapore 596224

*USA office:* 27 Warren Street, Suite 401-402, Hackensack, NJ 07601

*UK office:* 57 Shelton Street, Covent Garden, London WC2H 9HE

**British Library Cataloguing-in-Publication Data**
A catalogue record for this book is available from the British Library.

**Economic Growth Centre Research Monograph Series — Vol. 1**
**ECONOMIC GROWTH AND TRANSITION**
**Econometric Analysis of Lim's S-Curve Hypothesis**

ISBN-13 978-981-4291-83-5
ISBN-10 981-4291-83-8

Typeset by Stallion Press
Email: enquiries@stallionpress.com

Printed in Singapore.

For Yu Xuan and May Xuan

My beloved daughters

# Preface

Professor Lim Chong Yah's S-Curve hypothesis is a simple yet highly insightful theory. By augmenting the mathematical and econometrical sophistication of the hypothesis, this book extends the S-Curve hypothesis to provide further insights into economic growth and transition. The four core chapters in this book are closely related yet distinctly different, each dealing with a separate aspect of the S-Curve hypothesis.

Chapter 2 constructs a stochastic growth model that provides the microeconomic foundation for the S-Curve hypothesis. The model is based on the technological diffusion model by Barro and Sala-i-Martin (1997) with two significant extensions: the (productivity) parameter in the model, which represents social infrastructure, is being endogenized and the probability of adverse shocks is being incorporated into it. The stochastic technological diffusion model is able to explain the various transition points outlined in the S-Curve hypothesis. The model is also able to explain why some developing economies experience economic take-off, while others do not. The model highlights the importance of lowering the cost of technological absorption in enhancing growth rates of developing countries, and lowering the cost of innovation in achieving technological leadership. The model also highlights the importance of good governance in economic development and identifies negative shocks to governance as the main cause of slow growth in the poor developing countries.

Chapter 3 employs the economic transition parameter and the variance ratio test, developed by Phillips and Sul (2003, 2005), to test for convergence of the world economy under the framework of the S-Curve hypothesis. The results show that there is no evidence of overall convergence of the world economy. In addition, while there is evidence of subgroup convergence among the elephant economies, the horse economies and the turtle economies outside the African region, there is no sub-group convergence among the African turtle economies. While this is insufficient to conclude that there would be no ultimate convergence of the world economy, the results show that the poorest countries (especially those in the African region) are not catching up at all in the last 40–50 years.

Chapter 4 hypothesizes the accumulation of capital in an economy as it develops follows that of an S-Curve. A newly industrializing economy (NIE) would experience rapid accumulation of capital, with the growth of capital outstripping that of output, while a maturing economy would face a slow-down in capital growth. As a result, the incremental capital-output ratio (ICOR) and the average capital-output ratio (ACOR) would first increase and then gradually decline when a country ascends the development ladder. A rapidly developing economy would have high and increasing ICOR and ACOR. Cross-country data from 60 countries provides support to the hypothesis of the S-Curve of capital accumulation. In addition, a case study using Singapore's capital stock data from 1960 to 2006 also concurs with the hypothesis. The long-term causal relationship between Singapore's capital stock and its GDP was tested and found to be positive and bi-directional.

Chapter 5 applies the S-Curve hypothesis to the case studies of Japan and Singapore. Using Chow test, it is shown that Japan underwent a structural change in 1974 while Singapore underwent a structural change in 1997, as both countries began their transformation into an elephant economy. The case study of Japan concludes that the S-Curve hypothesis is able to explain the rapid growth of the Japanese economy in the 1950s and 1960s, and its eventual slow-down since the late 1980s. By comparing the macroeconomic indicators of Japan and Singapore, it is deduced that Singapore is at the initial phase of a gradual transformation to an elephant economy; the real per capita GDP of Singapore is expected to grow at an annual average of 3.5% to 4% in the next 20 years and slow down to 1.5% to 2% thereafter.

# Acknowledgments

I would like to thank Professor Lim Chong Yah, who was my PhD thesis supervisor, for being so generous in sharing his immense knowledge and valuable insights with me. He is my inspiration and role model. I am deeply privileged and honored to be his student.

I would also like to express my sincere thanks and gratefulness to the co-supervisor of my thesis, Associate Professor Shahidur Rahman, for his dedication, guidance and helpful advice. My gratitude also goes to Associate Professor Chen Kang, Associate Professor Mike Leu, Professor Ng Yew Kwang, and Professor Colin Kirkpatrick for their encouragement and constructive comments and suggestions. Finally, I would like to thank my husband, Lawrence, and my two beautiful daughters, Yu Xuan and May Xuan, for their understanding and love. I am also grateful to my parents and my parents-in-law, who have unselfishly provided me with family support, without which the completion of this monograph will not be possible. I am also grateful to Professor Euston Quah, head of Economic Division of NTU, for his generous support and assistance.

I would like to thank Tung Yue Nang, a celebrated Singapore artist, for photographing and designing the gorgeous book cover. We had a discussion on the photographic presentation of economic transition and decided that access to clean drinking water is a good marker for economic development.

SNG Hui Ying
February, 2009

# Contents

# List of Figures

# List of Tables

# List of Abbreviations

| | |
|---|---|
| ACOR | Average capital-output ratio |
| E (in EGOIN) | Entrepreneurship |
| G (in EGOIN) | Government |
| GCS | Gross capital stock |
| GDP | Gross domestic product |
| GDS | Gross domestic savings |
| GFCF | Gross fixed capital formation |
| I (in EGOIN) | (Accumulated) Investment |
| ICOR | Incremental capital-output ratio |
| N (in EGOIN) | Natural resources |
| NCS | Net capital stock |
| NIE | Newly industrializing economy |
| O (in EGOIN) | Ordinary labor |
| PIM | Perpetual inventory method |
| PPP | Purchasing power parity |
| TFP | Total factor productivity |

# CHAPTER 1

# Introduction and Overview

## 1.1. Introduction

The study of economic growth is broad and immense and its importance is indisputable. Barro and Sala-i-Martin (1995) show that small differential in growth rates, when compounded over long periods of time, resulted in dramatically different standards of living. Over the centuries, from Adam Smith (1776), David Ricardo (1817) and Thomas Malthus (1798), to the recent New Growth Theory by Grossman and Helpman (1991) and Aghion and Howitt (1992), economists seek to find answers to the questions, "what are the drivers of economic growth?", "what are the necessary factors for economic take-off?", and "what explains the differences in income levels across countries over time?"

The focus of this book is the extension of the work on development economics by Emeritus Professor Lim Chong Yah. In over 40 years as an academic researcher, Professor Lim preserves in his relentless pursuit of answers to the questions "how might poverty be alleviated?" and "how might affluence be achieved?" His decade-long efforts crystallized into the Trinity development model, encompassing the EGOIN theory, the Triple C theory and the S-Curve hypothesis (Lim, 2009). Professor Lim's Trinity development model seeks to provide utilizable solutions to poverty alleviation and economic development. It has the noble objective of providing a general formula for development that can be adopted by developing countries. Of the three theories within the Trinity development model, this book focuses on the mathematical and econometrical sophistication of the S-Curve hypothesis, although references will be made to the other two theories.

The structure of this chapter is as follows: Section 1.2 provides a review of the S-Curve hypothesis, and relates the S-Curve hypothesis to Lim's EGOIN theory and Triple C theory. The interpretations of the S-Curve are given in Section 1.3. Section 1.4 provides empirical support for the S-Curve hypothesis using empirical data and empirical conclusions presented by other researchers. The S-Curve hypothesis offers interesting insight and policy implications for economic development, and these are elaborated in Section 1.5.

## 1.2. Review of the S-Curve Hypothesis

### 1.2.1. *Brief description of the S-Curve hypothesis*

The S-Curve hypothesis, as shown in Fig. 1.1, classifies the world economy into three broad groups: turtle (low income, slow growth), horse (middle income, rapid growth), and elephant (high income, slow growth). The S-Curve is plotted with log per capita income on the $y$-axis and time on the $x$-axis. The growth rate of the per capita income is given by the slope of the S-Curve. Thus, the steeper the slope, the higher the growth rate. According to Lim (2009), in terms of per capita income growth rate, elephant economies normally grow at less than 3–4% per annum, whereas horse economies grow at more than 4%, at times much more than 4% per annum. Turtle economies, like elephants, will grow at 3–4% per annum at best.

Turtles move slowly, hiding beneath their shells. Turtle economies are plagued by low savings and investment rates, poor infrastructure, underdeveloped human resources and low quality of government. Many

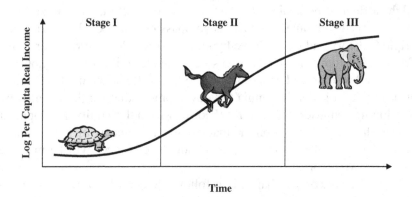

**Fig. 1.1.**   S-Curve of economic development.

of these countries are in the low-level equilibrium trap, where high population growth often wipes out any potential per capita income growth. Developing at a crawling pace, the income levels of these turtle economies diverge further and further away from the rest of the world.

Some, definitely not all, of these turtle economies would break away from the vicious poverty cycle and metamorphose into rapidly-developing horse economies. Horse economies are characterized by high savings rates, high private sector's investment rates (including foreign direct investment), high public sector's investment in physical and human capital, export-oriented industrializing policy, favorable investment climate, and a stable, pro-development government. The rapid growth rate enjoyed by the horse economies can be attributed to the high rate of capital accumulation undertaken by the public and private sectors. It can also be explained by the quantum-leap transfer of technology, organizational skills and production techniques from the developed nations, which were made possible by the relatively low level of development of the horse economies in addition to trade and investment openness.[1] Galloping at a superlative rate, the income levels of these horse economies converge towards those of the developed nations.

The elephant is a high consumption animal. It is big and it moves slowly. Economic success in the affluent countries has led to a decline in the marginal utility of money and an increase in the preference for leisure. People in these countries consume more, save less, and have higher marginal propensity to consume leisure. Many of these economies are also confronted with the problem of an aging population that has an adverse impact on the growth rates of these economies.[2] In addition, accumulated

---

[1] The basis that allows for quantum-leap improvement in productive capability is similar to that put forth by Ng and Yang (1999), although they have focused on division of labor as the determinant of organizational efficiency. According to them, a less developed country as a newcomer in the industrialization process can always "obtain free information on the efficient pattern of the division of labor". The less developed country can thus mimic the organization pattern that has been proven to be efficient in the developed economies. Hence, instead of a gradual evolution of the division of labor, it is possible for a big jump in industrialization to take place.

[2] GDP per capita can be expressed as a multiplicative relationship between average labor productivity and share of population employed: $Y/POP = Y/N \times N/POP$, where $Y$ is total output, $POP$ is total population, and $N$ is number of employed workers. An aging population would thus imply a decreasing share of population employed and put downward pressure on per capita GDP growth rate of the country.

capital stock is immense after many decades of physical development, resulting in diminishing marginal returns and relatively lesser investment opportunities for both the private and public sectors. Moreover, de-industrialization commonly takes place in the elephant economies as manufacturing activities are relocated to the cheaper developing economies. All these lead to a lower rate of investment. These factors, according to the S-Curve hypothesis, slow down economic growth.

Table 1.1 gives a comparison of the characteristics of the turtle, horse and elephant economies.

### 1.2.2.  *S-Curve and EGOIN theory*

The S-Curve hypothesis is closely associated with the EGOIN theory, another proposition by Lim (1984, 1991, 2009) that postulates the level of economic development of a country is a direct function of its EGOIN. EGOIN stands for the five domestic co-determinants of economic development: Entrepreneurship (E), Government (G), Ordinary Labor (O), Investment (I) and Natural Resources (N). EGOIN is both the source and the manifestation of growth in an economy. The higher the level of EGOIN, the higher the economy will be on the S-Curve. Economies with rapidly improving EGOIN would enjoy rapid growth, and these economies belong to the horse category. On the other hand, turtle economies are those with low and stagnant levels of EGOIN, and the EGOIN levels of elephant economies are very high but growing very slowly at the same time. The EGOIN theory distinguishes between rate and level of growth. In order to grow rapidly, economies need to improve steadily on their EGOIN. Economies that experience quantum-leap improvement in their EGOIN, for example a move from planned economies to market-oriented economies (E), or adoption of pro-development investment and trade policies (G, E, I), will enjoy a jump in their economic growth rates.

The EGOIN theory adopts a man-centred approach, where E, G and O are considered as the active agents of growth. EGO is also the social capacity of an economy to accumulate and utilize the available physical and natural resources. The theory puts human factors on center-stage and the aptitude and attitude of the government, with its accompanying bureaucracy, as the most important co-determinants of

**Table 1.1.** Characteristics of turtle, horse and elephant economies.

| | Turtle | Horse | Elephant |
|---|---|---|---|
| Income per capita | Low and slowly growing | Medium and rapidly growing | High and slowly growing |
| Savings rate | Low | High | Low |
| Investment rate | Low | High | Low |
| Openness to trade and investment | Low | High | High |
| Demographic profile | Usually high population growth | Youthful, usually controlled population growth | Aging population |
| Investment climate | Poor | Conducive | Diminishing returns and rising land and labor costs |
| Emphasis of society | Meeting basic needs and survival | Priority on economic achievements | High marginal propensity of leisure |
| Entrepreneurship | Poor, profusion of market-distorting government interventions | Market-oriented and entrepreneur-enabling | Market-oriented and entrepreneur-enabling |
| Government | Poor in both economic and political leaderships | Good leader with emphasis on economic development | Good leadership with emphasis on social development |
| Human capital | Underdeveloped | Medium and rapidly improving | High |
| Fixed capital accumulation | Poor infrastructures and low level of private sector capital accumulation | Rapidly improving infrastructures and rapid increase in private sector capital accumulation | Infrastructures and private sector capital stock well built up |
| Natural resources | Not well-utilized or lacking | Well-utilized | Well-utilized |

development. Two key features differentiate the EGOIN theory from many other development theories. Firstly, the EGOIN theory is multi-faceted. Secondly, it emphasizes on the human determinants of development, in particular the quality of government and its bureaucracy. The multi-causality of the EGOIN and its focus on government provide a higher degree of realism to the theory.

### 1.2.3. *S-Curve and Triple C theory*

The Triple C theory, also by Lim (1996, 2009), postulates that economic growth is propelled by three engines: the domestic, the regional and the global. The domestic engine is powered by the EGOIN of the economy, while the regional and global engines are lubricated by trade and invest-ment openness. Trade and investment are necessary for an economy to benefit from the inventions and technological advancement of other economies. Trade and investment also help to enlarge market size and enhance competitiveness. Thus, a (horse) economy that embraces open trade and investment policies stands to grow at a much higher rate than a (turtle) economy that adopts close trade and investment policies.

The Triple C theory argues that in order to drive the other two engines, it is necessary to have a domestic engine that functions well (Lim, 2009). If the domestic engine malfunctions, in particular "G", the regional and global engines will fail to work too. The importance of gov-ernment and its bureaucracy in harnessing the benefits of globalization has also been put forth by other researchers. As Kirkpatrick (1994) and Cook and Kirkpatrick (1997) point out, "deriving the potential benefits of globalization requires effective economic management and policy formulation on the part of national policy-makers. Where administra-tive, institutional and organizational structures are weak, the capacity to 'manage' the globalization process is undermined".

### 1.3. Interpretations of the S-Curve

### 1.3.1. *S-Curve as the development path of an economy*

The S-Curve can be used to portray the development path of an individ-ual economy. In this case, the variable on the *y*-axis will be the level of economic development with (log) per capita income commonly used as a proxy. The *x*-axis variable is time. The slope of the S-Curve gives the rate of growth of the per capita income $(d \ln Y(t)/dt = \dot{Y}(t)/Y(t))$.

It is noted that each country has its own unique S-Curve. The S-Curve only depicts the general pattern of development. It does not explicate the duration a country would remain as a turtle/horse economy. It also does not spell out the per capita income level of a matured elephant economy. Figure 1.2 gives an illustration of the differing development paths of three countries. Using Economy 1 as a baseline case and supposing all three economies experience take-off at about the same period, Economy 2 grows at a faster pace and is thus transformed into an elephant economy over a much shorter period of time. On the other hand, Economy 3 only manages to achieve a much lower level of per capita income as compared to Economy 1, when both economies are in their third stage of economic development. According to the EGOIN Theory, the growth rate of an economy is determined by the rate of improvement of its EGOIN, while the income level of an economy is determined by its level of EGOIN. In the case of Economy 2, the rapid improvement in its E, G, O, I and N explains its rapid transformation. In the case of Economy 3, constraints such as geographical location, political state of affairs, lack of natural resources and even culture and social norms — factors which are often not within the control of the leaders and the people of the country, could cap the potential income level of an economy.

It is also noted that the not all time plots of per capita income of economies would show an S-Curve. For instance, the time plots of

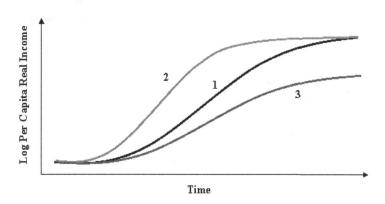

**Fig. 1.2.** Different S-Curves for different economies.

per capita income of turtle economies would not show an S-Curve, as these economies have not experienced economic take-off. In addition, the data series needs to be sufficiently long so as to trace the development of an economy. This will allow the time plot to show an S-Curve. Thus, limitation in the availability of data could result in the inability to sketch the S-Curve of the economic development of a country.

### 1.3.2. *S-Curve as a snapshot of the world economy*

The S-Curve can be used to depict a snapshot of the economic landscape of the world economy. In this case, the *y*-axis variable is the level of economic development while the *x*-axis represents the development stages, i.e. turtle, horse and elephant. Countries under study would be placed in ascending order according to their stages of development. The slope of the S-Curve represents the growth rates of the economies. Although it is not possible to plot the S-Curve in this context using empirical data, it is insightful to view the ranking of the economies against the framework of the S-Curve. Figure 1.3

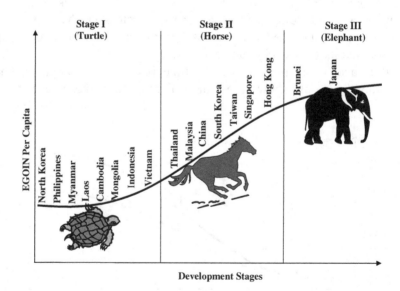

**Fig. 1.3.**   S-Curve for the 17 East Asian economies.

*Source*: Lim (2005).

shows the ranking of the 17 East Asian economies according to their EGOIN per capita by Lim (2005).[3,4]

## 1.4. Empirical Support of the S-Curve Hypothesis

The S-Curve hypothesis is well-supported by empirical data. This section presents three separate bodies of evidence of validity of the S-Curve hypothesis.

### 1.4.1. *Evidence 1: Relationship between long-term growth rate and per capita income level*

If the S-Curve hypothesis is correct, a graphical plot of long-run GDP per capita growth rate against GDP per capita would present itself as an inverted U-shaped curve — low growth rates at the two ends of the income spectrum, and high growth rates for the middle-income countries.

Figure 1.4 plots the average annual growth rates of GDP per capita of 115 countries over a period of 40 years from 1961–2000 against their respective GDP per capita in 1990. The data are obtained from the Penn World Table 6.1 (Heston, Summers *et al.*, 2002).[5] The GDP per capita figures are both PPP-adjusted and inflation-adjusted. The data series is fitted with a second order polynomial function with GDP per capita growth rates (*GYPC*) as the dependent variable and GDP per capita (*YPC*) as the explanatory variable. The result of the

---

[3] Some researchers may question the wisdom of placing Brunei as an Elephant economy. However, it is noted that the S-Curve in Fig. 1.3 is plotted against EGOIN per capita. Thus, what Brunei lacks in the quality of other aspects of EGOI is sufficiently made up through its abundance in oil and natural gas (N).

[4] GDP per capita has often been used as a proxy for EGOIN per capita. However, an important difference between the two measures is that while GDP is the output of a country, EGOIN measures the output potential of the country.

[5] Data on 168 countries are available from the PWT 6.1. However, only 115 countries have GDP per capita data spanning across more than 30 years. These 115 countries are used in the following analysis.

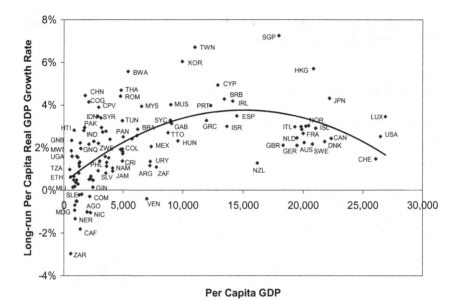

**Fig. 1.4.**  Average annual GDP per capita growth rate from 1961–2000 versus GDP per capita in 1990 (international $ in 1996 prices).

*Source*: Computed through data from PWT 6.1 (Heston, Summers *et al.*, 2002).

regression and the corresponding *t*-statistics (in parentheses) are given as follows:

$$GYPC = 0.00356 + (4.523 \cdot 10^{-6}) \cdot YPC - (1.501 \cdot 10^{-10}) \cdot (YPC)^2$$

$$\qquad\qquad (1.404) \qquad\qquad (6.426) \qquad\qquad\qquad (-5.036)$$

$$R^2 \quad = 0.3588$$

The coefficients for *YPC* and *YPC²* are significant and are correctly signed. The predicted values show an inverted U-shape in Fig. 1.4.

The U-shaped relationship between the GDP per capita growth rate and the GDP per capita can also be tested using the correlation coefficient: correlation between the two variables should be positive for low to medium per capita income level, and negative for high per capita income level. Using International $15,000 as a cut-off point, we tested for the correlation between the GDP per capita growth rate and the GDP per capita. For countries with per capita income below International $15,000, which would include the turtle and the horse economies, the Pearson product moment correlation coefficient is 0.59. On the other hand, for countries with per capita income above International $15,000, the Pearson product moment correlation coefficient is −0.09. Thus, the results support the S-Curve hypothesis again.

### 1.4.2. *Evidence 2: Growth patterns of country groups by income levels*

Phillips and Sul (2005) use per capita real income data from the Penn World Table from 1960 to 1996 to illustrate the growth patterns of 88 economies by income groups. The authors first divide the 88 countries into five sub-groupings based on their initial income: poorest, poor, middle, rich and richest. The authors then plot the time paths of the sub-group averages over five successive panels in the same graph, from the poorest to the richest. Each panel spans the 37-year period between 1960 and 1996. The resultant graphical plot, as given in Fig. 1.5, is an interesting and new way of looking at the evidence of convergence and growth. Equally interesting is that the graphical plot resembles Lim's S-Curve of

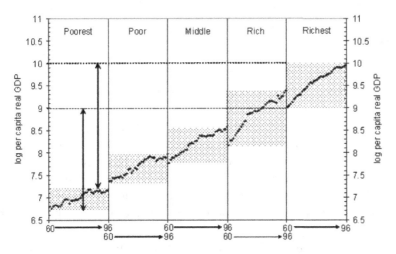

**Fig. 1.5.** World economic growth, 1960–1996.

*Source*: Phillips and Sul (2005).

economic development. Relating Figure 1.5 to Figure 1.1 of the S-Curve hypothesis, the "poorest" and "poor" country groups correspond to the "turtle economies", the "middle" and "rich" country groups correspond to the "horse economies", and the "richest" country group corresponds to the "elephant economies".

As described by Phillips and Sul (2005), "While each panel restarts the time profile from 1960 onwards, the arrangement of the panels produces an escalator effect from the poorest to the richest groups that is surprisingly connected in form. The escalator begins with a stair that has a fairly flat shape corresponding to the slow growth of the poorest nations and the stairs generally become steeper as the nation groups become richer and grow faster". The total economic growth over a 37-year time span for the average of each country group is given by the height of the shadowed area in Fig. 1.5. With the exception of the "richest" country group, the total economic growth of the first four groups correlate positively to the initial income levels of the groups. The growth of the "richest" country group is lower than that of the "rich" country group, although it is higher than the other three groups. This result concurs with the S-Curve hypothesis which states that middle-income countries grow more rapidly than low- and high-income countries.

Furthermore, it can be seen from Fig. 1.5 that the "rich" countries are catching up with the "richest" countries, signaling convergence at the upper-tier of the world economy. On the other hand, the rest of the world economies are diverging from the "rich" and "richest" countries in terms of income level.

### 1.4.3.  *Evidence 3: Cross-country income distribution*

The S-Curve hypothesis predicts that over time, the turtle economies would diverge further and further away from the rest of the world, while the horse economies would catch up with the elephant economies. When viewed against empirical data on cross-country income distribution, one would expect the overall spread of per capita income to increase over time, while the income distribution between the upper-middle and the high-income economies to narrow over time.

Durlauf and Quah (1999) developed some stylized facts on the properties of cross-country distribution of growth characteristics. Using data from the Summers–Heston V.6 database for the period 1960–1989, the authors show that the overall spread of per capita incomes increased over time, "the extremes appear to be diverging away from each other — with the poor becoming poorer, and the rich richer". This stylized fact is in line with the S-Curve hypothesis which postulates that the turtle economies would diverge further and further away from the rest of the world.

In addition, Durlauf and Quah (1999) also show that within clusters, there is a fall in the spread between the relatively rich countries. According to the authors, the income distance between the 85th and 95th percentiles was 0.98 times world per capita income in 1960–1964; this distance fell to 0.59 in 1985–1989. This stylized fact is again in line with the S-Curve hypothesis which postulates convergence at the upper-income level of the world economy.

## 1.5. Insight and Implications of the S-Curve Hypothesis

The S-Curve hypothesis offers several insight and policy implications for economic development:

1. Income levels of the horse economies would converge towards those of the elephant economies, while income levels of the turtle economies would diverge away from the rest of the world. Over time, the income differential between the world's richest countries and the world's second richest is expected to narrow, although the overall income distribution of the world economy would remain wide.

2. In the long process of world economic development, many of the horse economies would eventually graduate to become elephant economies, although the growth prospects of some of the horse economies may falter and these economies would slip back to become turtle economies. At the same time, there would be some turtle economies whose EGOIN has undergone significant improvements, and these economies would transform into horse economies.

3. The superlative growth rates of the horse economies can be explained by high investment rates and quantum leaps in technological transfer (Lim, 2005). The rapid accumulation of physical capital, from both domestic and foreign investment, would directly result in higher GDP and would generate higher output growth for the future. At the same time, the relatively low level of development of the horse economies enables the quantum-leap transfer of technology, organizational skills

and production processes from the developed nations. It is thus important for developing countries to adopt open trade and investment policies that encourage interaction and exchange with other countries.

4.  The superlative growth rates of the horse economies would eventually slow down as their income levels approach those of the elephant economies. This is because the quantum-leap benefits enjoyed by the horse economies through technological transfer would diminish as their technological levels approach those of the elephant economies. A country such as Japan that used to be a horse economy during those decades after the Second World War has seen its growth rate slow since the late 1980s. In other words, the slow-down of the Japanese economy can be explained by the S-Curve hypothesis. Following the same line of argument, Singapore's economy will soon be slowing down to the 2–4% growth rate similar to those of the developed nations. There is very little theoretical and empirical support that suggests a very high-income economy can continue to grow at a superlative rate over a prolonged period of time.

5.  The rapid-growing horse economy that is able to catch up with the developed nations in a span of a few decades is a fairly recent phenomenon. Globalization, world trade, cross-continent investment and international capital flow have provided the necessary impetus to spur the growth of poor but open economies. In other words, openness to trade and investment are two of the most critical determinants of economic development.

6.  Growth determinants are multi-faceted. Apart from investment (I) and technological transfer (closely associated with I) that are emphasized by the S-Curve hypothesis, the other determinants are E, O, G and N as outlined in the EGOIN Theory. Of these, G, the attitude and aptitude of the government and its bureaucracy, is the most important determinant. G plays the role of an enabler; without G, the accumulation, development and full utilization of E, O, I and N will be hampered. However, in contrast to the stability of the other four co-determinants, G is susceptible to large and sudden fluctuations that could derail the development process of the economy.

7.  The level of income of an economy is dependent on the level of its EGOIN. Likewise, the rate of growth of the economy is dependent on the rate of improvement of its EGOIN. An economy whose government is adopting pro-development policies, opening up its economy steadily to international trade and private investment (E), improving

its human capital (O) continuously, accumulating physical capital stock rapidly (I) and/or utilizing its natural resources efficiently (N) would enjoy a high rate of economic growth.

## 1.6. Conclusion

The S-Curve hypothesis, to a large extent, captures a snapshot of the current economic landscape accurately. Empirical analysis in Section 1.4.1 shows that the world's economies can be broadly classified into the three categories according to the S-Curve hypothesis.

The S-Curve hypothesis also describes the development experiences of economies that have rapidly developed after the Second World War adequately, such as Singapore, Japan and China. These countries have experienced an intense phase of rapid development over a 30 to 40-year period in recent decades. Two important factors were present during the rapid growth phase of these countries that greatly strengthened their growth intensity: (1) other highly developed nations that these countries could emulate; and (2) increased globalization that facilitated knowledge transfer. These two factors allowed the quantum-leap in technological level and accompanied high-income growth to take place. The S-Curve hypothesis, however, is less useful in describing the development experiences of the OECD economies.

It is important to note that the S-Curve hypothesis is not an iron law — it only depicts a tendency. For instance, the hypothesis does not imply that all horse economies will continue on the "sure path" to future economic development. Political instability, turn-about on pro-development policies, and a corrupted and inefficient bureaucracy could always derail the growth of a horse economy and even push it back to a turtle economy. The hypothesis also does not imply that an elephant economy would always remain as an elephant economy. If complacency sets in, even a developed country could regress to a developing country as well.

The S-Curve hypothesis is a useful theory that can be used to explain both convergence and divergence, and the formation of a convergence club in economic development. Lim (1996) has also succinctly described the defining characteristics of economies at the various stages of development. One of the contributions of the S-Curve hypothesis is that it highlights the drivers of growth that are needed for economic development.

The main weakness of the S-Curve hypothesis is that it lacks quantitative rigor. There is a lack of empirical proof of the S-Curve hypothesis and there is a lack of empirical analysis on the growth paths of economies at different stages of development. In addition, the completeness of the S-Curve hypothesis as a growth model is also hindered by its lack of micro-economic foundation. These weaknesses will be addressed in the following chapters.

# CHAPTER 2

# Microeconomic Foundation of the S-Curve Hypothesis: A Stochastic Technological Diffusion Model

## 2.1. Introduction

According to Lim's S-Curve hypothesis of economic development (1994, 1996, 1997), there are three critical transition points along the development path of a nation. A growth model that aims to depict the development paths of the world economies should be able to generate these three transition points as part of its results. The three transition points are:

1. *Transformation of turtle economy to horse economy*. The transformation of a turtle economy to a horse economy is not an automatic process. Some turtle economies manage to move on to the higher growth path, while others are caught in the low-level equilibrium trap. The key factor that initiates the transformation is a significant improvement in the social infrastructure, in particular, the quality of government and its bureaucracy.
2. *Superlative growth of horse economy*. Horse economies grow rapidly, at significantly higher growth rates than the developed economies over long period of time. These higher growth rates enable the horse economies to catch up with the developed economies in terms of per capita output level.
3. *Transformation of horse economy to elephant economy*. Matured economies grow slowly. Growth rates of the horse economies gradually slow down to approach those of the developed economies as the per capita output levels of the horse economies approach those of the developed economies.

In addition, the S-Curve hypothesis emphasizes the importance of technological transfer in spurring the growth of the horse economies. In this chapter, a stochastic technological diffusion model, extended from Barro and Sala-i-Martin's technological diffusion model (1997), is built to form the microeconomic foundation of the S-Curve hypothesis.

Barro and Sala-i-Martin (1997) construct a growth model that focuses on technological innovations in developed countries and technological diffusion to developing countries. In their model, long-run world growth is driven by discoveries in the advanced countries and technology diffusion takes place through the process of the developing countries copying the technological innovations of the developed nations. The lesser developed countries catch up with the developed countries since copying is cheaper than innovating, which allows the followers to grow at a faster rate. The growth rate of the follower countries eventually slows down as the costs of imitation increase with the diminishing pool of copiable materials. This gives rise to the pattern of conditional convergence, where the developing countries grow faster when they are further away from the developed nations. The major contribution of the Barro and Sala-i-Martin model stems from its ability to "combine elements of endogenous growth with the convergence implications of the neoclassical growth model". What is equally significant is that the model highlights the importance of technological innovations in world development and the importance of technological transfer in economic growth in the lesser developed countries.

However, the model is not without its shortcomings. In particular, an important parameter in the model that represents government policies and technological level is taken to be a constant and is exogenously determined. Barro and Sala-i-Martin term the parameter as the "productivity parameter". This parameter can also be taken as a measurement of the social infrastructure or social capacity of an economy. This exogeneity of the productivity parameter results in some difficulties in explaining economic transformation within the model. In particular, the model is not able to explain the transformation of a lesser developed economy that used to languish in slow growth to a fast-growing Newly Industrializing Economy (NIE). In addition, by treating the productivity parameter as a constant, the model ignores the positive causation between the productivity parameter and other aspects of development such as openness and technological advancement. The constancy of the productivity parameter also gives rise to the conclusion that rules out absolute convergence even in the long-run equilibrium. The model is also not able to explain why some lesser developed economies experience economic take-off while others do not.

This chapter aims to extend Barro and Sala-i-Martin's model by endogenizing the productivity parameter within the model. The productivity parameter is postulated to be an increasing function of economic linkages and technological advances. In addition, the improvement of productivity parameter is also postulated to be stochastic and influenced by "luck". These two extensions are both intuitive and are supported by empirical studies. Empirical research by Andersson (2001) and Bregman and Marom (1999) shows that openness contributes positively to productivity growth. In addition, analysis of Easterly *et al.* (1993) on the importance of "luck" in cross-country growth performance shows that "luck" is relatively important to policies in determining the long-run path of output.

The resultant model is a stochastic growth model that is able to explain the "catching up" of the NIEs with the advanced economies; the "slowing down" of the maturing NIEs and the slower growth rate of the developed economies; and the "lagging behind" of the poor developing economies. The model is also able to generate results that illustrate why some developing economies experience economic take-off while others do not. Technology diffusion is modeled as the determinant of conditional convergence of the NIEs, while technological progress and economic openness further strengthen the social infrastructure of the economy. This brings about absolute convergence. The model also highlights the importance of good governance in economic development and identifies negative shocks to governance as the main cause of slow growth of the poor developing countries (Sng *et al.*, 2009).

The structure of this chapter is as follows: Section 2.2 discusses the strengths and weaknesses of Barro and Sala-i-Martin's technological diffusion model in depicting general development path. Section 2.3 formulates the productivity parameter, while Section 2.4 describes the stochastic technological diffusion model with endogenized productivity parameter. Section 2.5 discusses the key results of the model and Section 2.6 provides the conclusion.

## 2.2. Barro and Sala-i-Martin's Technological Diffusion Model

To facilitate discussion of Barro and Sala-i-Martin's model, references will be made to several variables. The production function used in the model is given by:

$$Y_i = A_i \cdot L_i^{1-\alpha} \cdot \sum_{j=1}^{N_i} (X_{ij})^{\alpha}.$$

In the model, there are two countries, denoted by the index $i = 1,2$. Country 1 is the technological leader while country 2 is the follower. $A_i$ is a productivity parameter that represents various aspects of government policy such as taxation, provision of public services, and maintenance of property rights and level of technology. $L_i$ is labor input. $X_{ij}$ is the quantity employed of the $j$th type of nondurable intermediate good. $N_i$ is the number of types of intermediate goods available in country $i$. $\alpha$ is a constant between 0 and 1. The production function specifies diminishing marginal productivity of each input, such that $\partial Y_i / \partial X_{ij} > 0$, $\partial^2 Y_i / \partial X_{ij}^2 < 0$, and constant returns to scale in all inputs together. Technological progress takes the form of an expansion of the number of varieties of intermediate goods, which is captured by $N_i$. Similar setups have been used in Barro (1995), Romer (1990) and Rivera-Batiz and Romer (1991). The intrinsically superior country, in terms of high $A$, high $L$ and low cost of innovation, will be the technological leader; all inventions of new types of intermediate goods occur in this country. The intrinsically inferior country will be the follower; it imitates the intermediate goods available in the leader country and does not invent anything.

### 2.2.1. *Descriptive properties of the model*

Through the assumptions that copying is cheaper than innovating, and that the costs of copying increase as the pool of copiable materials diminishes, Barro and Sala-i-Martin's technology diffusion model is able to explain the rapid growth of the newly industrializing economies (NIEs) and the slowing down of these economies as they mature. In other words, the result exhibits conditional convergence, where the developing countries grow faster when they are further away from the developed nations. It is also able to explain why advanced economies grow at a slower rate as compared to the NIEs, and thus allowing the NIEs to catch up with the advanced economies. In addition, the model allows for the case where a developing country grows at a slower pace than the developed country, such that divergence actually takes place and the developing country lags behind. In their model, if the ratio of the productivity parameters of the two countries $(A_2/A_1)$ is low, such that the steady state ratio of per-worker outputs $(\dot{y}_2/y_1)^*$ is small, then the growth rate of the developing country $(\dot{y}_2/y_2)$ can be below the growth rate of the advanced economy $(\dot{y}_1/y_1)$ even if $y_2$ is substantially less than $y_1$. In other words, (conditional) convergence does not necessarily take place in the model.

### 2.2.2.  *Inadequacy of the model in describing economic development*

Barro and Sala-i-Martin's (1997) model explains the second and third transition points of an economy adequately, as listed in Section 2.1, with the exception that the model is not able to generate a convergence in per capita output level. In the model, growth rate equalizes but not the income level at the steady state. A country that was initially a follower will be a perpetual follower.

In addition, while the model allows for the case of a slow-growing, low-income economy, it cannot explain why some developing economies take off, while others are left behind. Furthermore, a developing country that is initially growing slower than the developed country will always be a laggard, and there is no mechanism for it to be transformed into a fast-growing economy at all.

These results are at odds with the empirical evidence. Studies by Hsiao and Hsiao (2004) and Cunado, Gil-Alana and Perez de Gracia (2004) show that real GDP per capita of NIEs (Taiwan and Korea) are converging to that of developed nations (Japan and United States). In addition, Hsiao and Hsiao (2004) also show that there are many historical examples of catching-up and falling-behind among nations. Similarly, there are also many examples of slow-growing turtle economies taking off and transforming into fast-growing horse economies.

Barro and Sala-i-Martin attempt to overcome these two shortfalls by assuming exogenous changes in the productivity parameter $A$. Thus, a slow-growing developing country can be transformed into a fast-growing developing country if there is an exogenous improvement in $A$. Similarly, a follower country can *over take* a leader country in terms of per worker output level if there is an exogenous improvement in $A$.

The productivity parameter $A$ in the model, which is taken to represent various aspects of government policy such as taxation, provision of public services, and maintenance of property rights and level of technology, is assumed to be constant and exogenous. These assumptions pose less of a constraint for the developed countries, but can be very problematic for the developing counties. The endogeneity of the productivity parameter $A$ will be discussed further in the following subsection.

The third but related shortcoming of the Barro and Sala-i-Martin's model is that it models economic development of the developing countries to depend only on technological transfer. The developing countries in the model catch up with the developed countries via imitation while the productivity parameter $A$ is assumed to remain constant. This assumption disregards the positive impact that foreign direct investment, trade, openness and technological transfer have on $A$. Thus, growth of the developing countries would be more rapid than predicted by Barro and Sala-i-Martin's model.

## 2.3. Interpretation and Enhancement of the Productivity Parameter

### 2.3.1. *Productivity parameter and EGOIN theory*

The productivity parameter $(A)$ in the Barro and Sala-i-Martin model (1997) is taken to represent various aspects of government policies and, to a lesser extent, level of technology. Technological progress in the model actually takes the form of an expansion of the number of varieties of intermediate goods, rather than an improvement in $A$. The use of $A$ in Barro and Sala-i-Martin's model is thus quite different from that in the usual Solow growth model (1956).

Comparing Barro and Sala-i-Martin's model to Lim's (1984, 1991, 2009) EGOIN Theory, improvement in $A$ is similar to improvement in $G$ in the EGOIN theory. EGOIN stands for Entrepreneurship (E), Government (G), Ordinary Labor (O), Investment (I), and Natural Resources (N). According to the EGOIN theory, the level of economic development of a country is a direct function of its EGOIN. According to the S-Curve hypothesis, the EGOIN of a developing economy has to be substantially improved before the economy can experience a take-off. Out of five determinants of the development of EGOIN, $G$ is the most important.[1] $G$ in the EGOIN theory is broadly defined. It includes policy orientation of the government, protection of property rights, maintenance of law and order, control of corruption and efficiency and effectiveness of its bureaucracy in implementing the policies. In other words, $G$ encompasses the social infrastructure of the economy that allows productive activities to take place. In the following discussion, $A$ (and $G$) are taken to represent social infrastructure.

### 2.3.2. *Endogeneity of productivity parameter A*

The improvement in $A$ (or $G$) and its positive impact on economic development is likely to be reinforced. For example, a government of a developing economy, which could be new or incumbent, has a change in policy orientation and adopted pro-development policies such as openness in trade and foreign investment. Provided that the country is politically stable and the cost of operation is reasonably low, the country is likely to experience an influx of foreign investment, an increase in international trade, and advancement in economic development. The increased interaction with the global market is likely to have positive impact on $A$ (or $G$) in the medium to long-term in areas such as the judiciary system, property rights protection, organization of the bureaucracy, and so on. These improvements in the various aspects of $A$ (or $G$) will further increase the attractiveness of the country as a destination of investment and enhance the competitiveness of exports.

In the context of Barro and Sala-i-Martin's model, technological progress is modeled as an expansion of the varieties of the intermediate goods. Developing economies import technological know-how from the developed nations. Implicit in the model is the assumption that there is openness to trade and investment in the developing economies. As the developing economies "learn" new technological know-how from the developed economies, they also "learn" better ways of organizing their

---

[1] The importance of a good and pro-development government in economic development is also echoed by other researchers such as Fukuyama (2004) and Kaufmann (2006). Kaufmann, the Director of Global Governance at the World Bank Institute, was quoted as saying that good governance is the "300% development dividend".

bureaucracy, conducting their macro economic policies and managing their economies. In other words, $A$ cannot be constant as $N$ increases, i.e. $A$ has to be an increasing function of $N$.

There are two implications of $A$ being an increasing function of $N$. Firstly, absolute convergence between the NIEs and the developed nations is a real possibility. The NIEs could catch up with the developed nations not only in terms of growth rates, but also in terms of income levels. Secondly, the NIEs have grown at superlative rates not only because of technological advancement, but also improvement in policies, institutions, and organization structure. Thus, the growth rates of the developing countries would be more rapid than those predicted by Barro and Sala-i-Martin's model.

### 2.3.3. *Role of chance in the productivity parameter*

If $A$ is taken to represent the encompassing role of $G$, then "chance" will be one of the factors that affects improvement in $A$. A similar view had also been expressed by Professor Arthur Lewis. Huang (2005), a former director of the World Bank, recounted a conversation with Professor Arthur Lewis where he asked Professor Lewis, "why do some developing countries grow faster than others?" Professor Lewis answered, "great leader and good policies ... however the emergence of a Great Man and the emergence of good policies seem to be largely a matter of luck". The comment by Professor Lewis has to be augmented further. Firstly, the "emergence of a Great Man" can and should be generalized to the "emergence of a good government". Secondly, a "good government" that facilitates and enables economic development is one that is market-oriented and development-oriented.

There are many examples that show how luck plays an important role in determining the transformation of a turtle economy to a horse economy, such as Singapore and China. There are even more examples of developing countries plagued by the bad luck of having bad leadership, or good leaders but bad polices. These countries either fail to take off, or if they manage to take off, say due to abundance of natural resources, they are likely to eventually suffer a growth reversal or stagnation.

The improvement of $A$ is likely to be influenced by chance. This probability of improvement is also likely to increase together with economic development. As compared to a well-developed elephant economy, a turtle economy with ill-defined and poorly-secured property rights, weak legislative frameworks and inefficient bureaucracy is more exposed to abuse by bad leadership and more likely to encounter bad policies or failure to implement good polices. This postulation is supported with empirical evidence by Quah (1993) and Acemoglu and Zilibotti (1997). Quah (1993) shows that the probability of adverse shocks to national incomes decreases as the national incomes increase. Acemoglu and Zilibotti (1997) show that poor countries exhibit considerably higher variability of output than more developed economies, thus giving support to the claim that "the process of development is perilous at the early stages".

### 2.3.4. *Formulation of the productivity parameter*

Let country 1 in the model represent the developed nations. The productivity parameter $A_1$ of country 1 is postulated to be an increasing function of technological advancement, $N_1$. Furthermore, as the social infrastructure of the country 1 is well-developed, we postulate that $A_1$ is not affected by luck. For tractability, we assume $A_1$ to take on the following functional form:

$$A_1 = f(N_1) = N_1^\beta, \quad A_1'(N_1) > 0, \quad A_1''(N_1) < 0, \quad \beta < 1, \quad (1)$$

where $A_1'$ and $A_1''$ are the first and second order differentials of $A_1$.

Country 2 in the model represents the developing economy. As discussed in the earlier section, it is postulated that the productivity parameter of country 2, $A_2$, is an increasing function of technological advancement, $N_2$, and it is influenced by chance. Again, for tractability, we assume $A_2$ to take on the following functional form:

$$A_2 = \Theta \cdot f(N_2) = \Theta \cdot N_2^\beta, \quad A_2'(N_2) > 0, \quad A_2''(N_2) < 0, \quad \beta < 1, \quad (2)$$

where $\Theta$ is the stochastic component of $A_2$. $N_2$ is an indicator of technological advancement of country 2; $N_2$ also serves as a proxy of the level of linkages country 2 has with the advanced economy.

If both country 1 and country 2 share the same functional form, the productivity parameter of country 2 can be written as:

$$A_2 = \Theta A_1 \left( \frac{N_2}{N_1} \right)^{\beta}, \qquad \beta < 1 \tag{3}$$

$\Theta$ is the stochastic component of $A_2$, which is influenced by luck. $\Theta$ is a random variable which can take two values, $0 < \Theta^L < \Theta^H = 1$. The productivity parameter of country 2 is subjected to a random shock every period. In the event of a positive shock, $\Theta = \Theta^H = 1$ and $A_2 = A_1 (N_2/N_1)^{\beta}$. In the event of a negative shock, $\Theta = \Theta^L < 1$, and $A_2 < A_1 (N_2/N_1)^{\beta}$. For simplicity, it is assumed that all $\Theta_t^L$ are the same $(=\Theta^L)$ and all $\Theta_t^H$ are the same $(=\Theta^H)$.

It is further postulated that as the social infrastructure of the economy becomes better developed, such that $A_{2t+1} > A_{2t}$, the likelihood of an occurrence of negative shock decreases. This assumption can be understood in two ways. Firstly, an advanced economy with its checks and balances in place, is less likely to be hijacked by "bandits" (Olson, 1993). Secondly, an economy with its social infrastructure well-built up is less susceptible to the occasional bad policies implemented by a well-intentioned government.

Let $p_t$ be the probability of appearance of good government and/or good policies:

$$p_t \equiv \Pr(\Theta_t = \Theta^H). \tag{4}$$

Recall from the earlier discussion, this probability, $p_t$, is an increasingly function of (last period) $A_2$. We further postulate that as the country becomes well-developed, such that $A_2$ approaches $A_1$, $p$ approaches 1. This assumption stems from our earlier assumption that $A_1$ is not subjected to shock. Thus:

$$p_t = g(A_{2t-1}), \quad g'(A_{2t-1}) > 0. \tag{5}$$

The expected value of $\Theta$ at time $t$ is given by:

$$E(\Theta_t) = \theta_t = (1 - p_t) \cdot \Theta^L + p_t \cdot \Theta^H = (1 - p_t) \cdot \Theta^L + p_t \tag{6}$$

$E(\Theta)$ approaches 1 as the country becomes well-developed.

From equation (3), if the technological level of country 2 catches up with that of country 1, such that $N_2/N_1$ tends to 1 in distribution, and $\Theta$ tends to 1 in probability, then using the Slutsky Theorem, $A_2$ tends to $A_1$ in distribution.

The schematic presentation of the relationship between $A_2$, $N_2$ and $p$ is shown as follows:

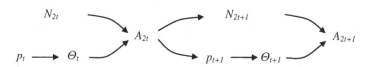

Thus, in period $t$, the (realized) values of $N_{2t}$ and $p_t$ will jointly determine the value of $A_{2t}$. The value of $A_{2t}$ will in turn influence the values of $N_{2t+1}$ and $p_{t+1}$. The effect of $A_{2t}$ on $N_{2t+1}$ will be further illustrated in Section 2.4.5.

## 2.4. The Stochastic Technological Diffusion Model

The basic model used in this section is largely drawn from Barro and Sala-i-Martin (1997). In this model, the basic model is extended with further characterization of the productivity parameter, $A$ (Sng *et al.*, 2009).

### 2.4.1. *Setup of the model*

In Barro and Sala-i-Martin's (1997) model, there are two countries, denoted by $i = 1, 2$. The production function in each country is:

$$Y_i = A_i \cdot L_i^{1-\alpha} \cdot \sum_{j=1}^{N_i} (X_{ij})^{\alpha}. \tag{7}$$

The variables are as defined under Section 2.2. The social infrastructure $A_i$ is accessible by all agents in country $i$, and production of the final goods occurs under competitive condition. Other assumptions include balanced trade and constant $L_i$. Each unit of consumption ($C_i$) or each unit of production of intermediate goods ($X_{ij}$) require one unit of $Y_i$. The invention of a new variety of product requires a lump-sum outlay of $\eta_i$ of $Y_i$. $\eta_i$ assumed to be constant, meaning that diminishing returns does not apply to invention.

### 2.4.2. *Innovation in country 1*

Country 1 is the technological leader initially, such that $N_1(0) > N_2(0)$, where 0 in the parenthesis refers to $t = 0$. As discussed earlier, $N_i$ measures the number of types of intermediate goods available in country $i$; it serves as an indicator of technological advancement of country $i$; The leading country is the innovator, and technological progress is displayed as an expansion of the number of varieties of intermediate goods.

The production function of country 1 is as follows:

$$Y_1 = A_1 \cdot L_1^{1-\alpha} \cdot \sum_{j=1}^{N_1} (X_{1j})^\alpha. \tag{8}$$

Inventor of an intermediate good $j$ retains a perpetual monopoly over the use of the intermediate good for production in country 1. The cost of invention is a constant $\eta_1$. The flow of monopoly profit to the inventor is expressed as:

$$\pi_{1j} = (P_{1j} - 1) \cdot (X_{1j}), \tag{9}$$

where $P_{1j}$ is the price of intermediate good $j$ in country 1, and 1 inside the parenthesis is the marginal cost of production for the intermediate good.

From equation (8), the marginal product of intermediate good $j$ is given by:

$$MP_{X_{1j}} = \frac{\partial Y_1}{\partial X_{1j}} = A_1 \cdot \alpha \cdot L_1^{1-\alpha} \cdot (X_{1j})^{\alpha-1}. \tag{10}$$

Equating this marginal product to the price of intermediate good $j$ ($P_{1j}$) gives the demand function for intermediate good $j$ from all producers of final goods in country 1 in the form:

$$X_{1j} = L_1 \cdot \left( \frac{A_1 \alpha}{P_{1j}} \right)^{1/(1-\alpha)}. \tag{11}$$

Substituting the demand function of intermediate good $j$ into equation (9) and maximizing profit with respect to $P_{1j}$ yields the monopoly price, which happens to be a constant and is the same for all intermediate goods $j$:

$$P_{1j} = P_1 = \frac{1}{\alpha} > 1. \tag{12}$$

Substituting the monopoly price into the demand function gives the total quantity of intermediate goods $j$ produced in country 1, which is the same for all intermediate goods $j$ but increases over time as $A_1$ improves:

$$X_{1j} = X_1 = L_1 \cdot (A_1)^{1/(1-\alpha)} \cdot \alpha^{2/(1-\alpha)}. \tag{13}$$

Substituting expression of $P_1$ from equation (12) and $X_1$ from equation (13) into the profit flow equation (9), we derive:

$$\pi_{1j} = \pi_1 = (1-\alpha) \cdot L_1 \cdot (A_1)^{1/(1-\alpha)} \alpha^{(1+\alpha)/(1-\alpha)}. \tag{14}$$

Profit is the same for all intermediate goods $j$ but increases over time as $A_1$ improves.

If there is free entry to the R&D business and the equilibrium quantity of R&D is non-zero at each point in time, then the present value of profits at time $t$ must equal the constant cost of invention, say $\eta_1$, at each point in time. The present value of profits from date $t$ onwards is:

$$V_1(t) = \int_t^\infty \pi_{1t} \exp\left[ -\int_t^s r_1(v) \cdot dv \right] \cdot ds = \eta_1 \tag{15}$$

where $r_1(v)$ is the rate of return at time $v$.

Differentiate both sides of equation (15) with respect to $t$ and solve for $r_1$ to obtain:

$$r_{1t} = \frac{\pi_{1t}}{\eta_1} - \frac{\int_t^\infty \dot{\pi}_{1t} \cdot \exp\left[-\int_t^s r_1(v) \cdot dv\right] ds}{\eta_1}. \tag{16}$$

Thus, $r_1$ is the ratio of profit flow $(\pi_1)$ to the cost of invention $(\eta_1)$ minus the present value of change in profit. The change in profit arises due to the increase in the quantity of $X_1$ used in the production function, which in turn is due to the improvement in $A_1$ as $N_1$ increases. It is postulated in equation (1) that improvement in $A_1$ due to increase in $N_1$ encounters diminishing returns. If we assume level of $A_1$ is sufficiently high such that further improvement in $A_1$ as $N_1$ increases is negligible, then $\pi_{1t}$ is almost a constant and the second term in equation (16) approaches zero and we have $r_1$ as a constant:

$$r_1 = \frac{\pi_1}{\eta_1}. \tag{17}$$

The total output of country 1 is given by:

$$Y_1 = (A_1)^{1/(1-\alpha)} \cdot \alpha^{2\alpha/(1-\alpha)} \cdot L_1 N_1. \tag{18}$$

Thus, output per worker in country 1 increases with the productivity parameter, $A_1$, and the number of intermediate goods, $N_1$, i.e.:

$$y_1 \equiv \frac{Y_1}{L_1} = (A_1)^{1/(1-\alpha)} \cdot \alpha^{2\alpha/(1-\alpha)} \cdot N_1. \tag{19}$$

Consumers in country 1 are of the Ramsey type with infinite horizons. The number of consumers remains constant over time. Maximization of utility, subject to standard budget constraints, gives the growth rate of consumption as:

$$\frac{\dot{C}_1}{C_1} = \left(\frac{1}{\zeta}\right) \cdot (r_1 - \rho), \tag{20}$$

where $\zeta$ is the coefficient of relative risk aversion and $\rho$ is the rate of time preference. Since $r_1$ is taken to be a constant at high level of $A_1$ (or $Y_1$), the growth of $C_1$ is also constant.

In the full equilibrium, $N_1$ and $Y_1$ always grow at the same rate as $C_1$. If $\gamma_1$ denotes this common growth rate, then:

$$\gamma_1 = \left(\frac{1}{\zeta}\right) \cdot (r_1 - \rho) = \left(\frac{1}{\zeta}\right) \cdot \left(\frac{\pi_1}{\eta_1} - \rho\right). \qquad (21)$$

### 2.4.3. *Imitation in country 2*

Country 2 is the technological laggard initially, such that $N_1(0) > N_2(0)$. The copying and adaptation of one of country 1's intermediate goods for use in country 2 requires a lump-sum outlay, $v_2(t)$. It is assumed that $v_2(0) < \eta_2$, so imitation is initially more attractive than innovation for country 2. Barro and Sala-i-Martin (1997) reason that while cost of innovation could be taken as constant (as the number of potential inventions is unbounded), cost of imitation is likely to increase as the available pool of copiable materials decreases. Thus, $v_2$ is assumed to be an increasing function of $N_2/N_1$, i.e.:

$$v_2 = v_2\left(\frac{N_2}{N_1}\right), \quad v_2' > 0. \qquad (22)$$

In addition, Barro and Sala-i-Martin (1997) also assume the cost of imitation ($v_2$) approaches the cost of innovation ($\eta_2$) when $N_2/N_1$ approaches 1. When $N_2/N_1$ is equal or greater than 1, country 2 will opt to innovate rather than imitate, and the cost of increasing $N$ is equal to the constant $\eta_2$.

The production function of country 2 is as follows:

$$Y_2 = A_2 \cdot L_2^{1-\alpha} \cdot \sum_{j=1}^{N_2} (X_{2j})^\alpha \qquad (23)$$

$$\Rightarrow \quad Y_2 = \Theta A_1 \left(\frac{N_2}{N_1}\right)^\beta \cdot L_2^{1-\alpha} \cdot \sum_{j=1}^{N_2} (X_{2j})^\alpha, \qquad (24)$$

where $p_t \equiv \Pr(\Theta_t = \Theta^H) = g(A_{t-1})$, $g'(A_{t-1}) > 0$.

The expected output of country 2 is:

$$E(Y_2) = \theta A_1 \left( \frac{N_2}{N_1} \right)^{\beta} \cdot L_2^{1-\alpha} \cdot \sum_{j=1}^{N_2} \left[ E(X_{2j}) \right]^{\alpha}$$

$$= \tilde{A}_2 \cdot L_2^{1-\alpha} \cdot \sum_{j=1}^{N_2} \left[ E(X_{2j}) \right]^{\alpha}. \tag{25}$$

where $\theta = p + (1-p) \cdot \Theta^L$, and $\tilde{A}_2 = E(A_2) = \theta A_1 \left( \dfrac{N_2}{N_1} \right)^{\beta}$.

### 2.4.3.1.  *Imitators of intermediate goods and producers of final goods*

An agent pays $v_2(t)$ to imitate the $j$th variety of intermediate good from country 1. This agent is assumed to retain a perpetual monopoly right over the use of the intermediate good for production in country 2. The expected flow of profit to the agent is given by:

$$E(\pi_{2j}) = [E(p_{2j}) - 1] \cdot E(X_{2j}) \tag{26}$$

$E(P_{2j})$ is the expected price of intermediate good $j$ in country 2, and 1 inside the parenthesis is the marginal cost of production for the intermediate good.

The expected marginal product of intermediate good $j$ can be obtained by differentiating the production function in equation (25) with respect to $E(X_{2j})$:

$$E(MP_{X_{2j}}) = \frac{\partial E(Y_2)}{\partial E(X_{2j})} = \tilde{A}_2 \cdot \alpha \cdot L_2^{1-\alpha} \cdot \left[ E(X_{2j}) \right]^{\alpha-1}. \tag{27}$$

The demand function for intermediate good $j$ from all producers of goods in country 2 can then be obtained by equating the expected marginal product to the expected price of intermediate good $j$ in country 2:

$$E(X_{2j}) = \left[ \frac{\tilde{A}_2 L_2^{1-\alpha} \alpha}{E(P_{2j})} \right]^{1/(1-\alpha)}. \tag{28}$$

Substituting the demand function of intermediate good $j$ into equation (26) and maximizing profit with respect to $E(P_{2j})$ yields the monopoly price, which happens to be a constant and is the same for all intermediate goods $j$ and:

$$E(P_{2j}) = P_2 = \frac{1}{\alpha} > 1. \tag{29}$$

Substituting the monopoly price into the demand function equation (28) gives the expected total quantity of intermediate good $j$ produced in country 2, which is the same for all intermediate goods $j$ but increases over time as $\tilde{A}_2$ improves:

$$E(X_{2j}) = E(X_2) = L_2(\tilde{A}_2)^{1/(1-\alpha)}\alpha^{2/(1-\alpha)}. \tag{30}$$

Substituting expression of $P_2$ from equation (29), and $E(X_2)$ from equation (30) into the expected profit flow equation (26), we derive:

$$E(\pi_{2j}) = E(\pi_2) = (1-\alpha) \cdot L_2 \cdot (\tilde{A}_2)^{1/(1-\alpha)} \cdot \alpha^{(1+\alpha)/(1-\alpha)}. \tag{31}$$

Expected profit is the same for all intermediate goods $j$, but increases over time as $\tilde{A}_2$ increases. The present value of profits from date $t$ onwards is:

$$V_2(t) = \int_t^\infty \pi_{2t} \exp\left[-\int_t^s r_2(v) \cdot dv\right] \cdot ds, \tag{32}$$

where $r_2(v)$ is the rate of return at time $v$. If there is free entry into the imitation business, then $V_2(t)$ will be equal to the cost of imitation and:

$$V_2(t) = v_2\left(\frac{N_2}{N_1}\right). \tag{33}$$

Substitute equation (33) into equation (32) and differentiate both sides of the equation with respect to $t$ to solve for $r_2$:

$$\dot{v}_2(t) = -\pi_{2t} \cdot \exp - \int_t^t r_2(v) \cdot dv + \int_t^\infty \dot{\pi}_{2t} \cdot \exp\left[-\int_t^s r_2(v) \cdot dv\right] ds$$

$$+ \int_t^\infty \pi_{2t} \cdot \exp\left[-\int_t^s r_2(v) \cdot dv\right] \cdot r_2(v) ds$$

$$= -\pi_{2t} + \int_t^\infty \dot{\pi}_{2t} \cdot \exp\left[-\int_t^s r_2(v) \cdot dv\right] ds + r_2(v) \cdot v_2$$

$$r_2 = \frac{\pi_{2t}}{v_2} + \frac{\dot{v}_2}{v_2} - \frac{\int_t^\infty \dot{\pi}_{2t} \cdot \exp\left[-\int_t^s r_2(v) \cdot dv\right] ds}{v_2}. \tag{34}$$

Thus, $r_2$ includes the ratio of profit flow ($\pi_2$) to the cost of imitation ($v_2$), the capital-gain term ($\dot{v}_2/v_2$), and the present value of change in profit. It is noted that both $\pi_2$ and $v_2$ increase as $\tilde{A}_2$ (and $N_2/N_1$) increases, $\dot{v}_2/v_2$ is positive, and

$$\int_t^\infty \dot{\pi}_{2t} \cdot \exp\left[-\int_t^s r_2(v) \cdot dv\right] ds$$

is positive. The path of $r_2$ over the course of economic development is not definite.

The producers of final goods employ $L_2$ workers at wage rate $w_2$ and pay $P_2$ for intermediate goods $j$. Since these producers are competitive, they take $w_2$ and $P_2$ as given. Thus $w_2$ is given by the expected marginal product of labor as:

$$w_2 = E(MP_{L_2})$$

$$= \frac{\partial E(Y_2)}{\partial E(L_2)}$$

$$= (1-\alpha) \cdot \tilde{A}_2 \cdot L_2^{-\alpha} \cdot \sum_{j=1}^{N_i} (X_{2j})^\alpha$$

$$= (1-\alpha) \cdot \frac{E(Y_2)}{L_2}. \tag{35}$$

## 2.4.3.2. *Representative consumer*

Consumers in country 2 are of the Ramsey type with infinite horizons. The number of consumers is assumed to be constant over time. The household utility function takes the form:

$$U_2 = E_0 \int_{t=0}^{\infty} e^{-\rho t} \cdot \frac{C_2(t)^{1-\zeta} - 1}{1-\zeta} dt, \tag{36}$$

where $\rho > 0$ is the rate of time preference and $E_0$ is the expectation operator at $t = 0$. In this,

$$\frac{C_2(t)^{1-\zeta} - 1}{1-\zeta}$$

is the instantaneous utility function of each consumer at a given date, and $\zeta > 0$ is the coefficient of relative risk aversion. Consumers earn expected rate of return $E(r_2)$ on assets and receive the expected wage rate $E(w_2)$ on the fixed aggregate quantity of labor $L_2$. Total consumers' assets at time $t$ are equal to the market value of the firms, which is given by $v_2(t)N_2(t)$. Thus, the consumers' aggregate income is $w_2 L_2 + r_2 v_2 N_2$.

Because of the uncertainty, the consumers do not choose deterministic paths for consumption. Their choice of consumption at any date depends on all the shocks to $A_2$ and the effects on other variables up to the date. We use Euler equation to solve for the consumers' optimization behavior under uncertainty.[2] Consider the consumers in period $t$. Supposing they reduce consumption by a small amount $\Delta C$, investing this additional saving for a short period of time $\Delta t$, and then consuming the proceeds at time $t + \Delta t$. If the consumers are optimizing, the material impact of this change on lifetime utility must be zero.

Given the utility function, the marginal utility of $C(t)$ is $e^{-\rho t}C(t)^{-\zeta}$. Thus, the reduction of consumption by $\Delta C$ has a utility cost of $e^{-\rho t}C(t)^{-\zeta}\Delta C$.

---

[2] Subscript "2", which refers to country 2, is dropped from the following derivation in an attempt to simplify the presentation.

Since the expected instantaneous rate of return is $E[(r(t)]$, $C$ at time $t + \Delta t$ can be increased by $e^{E(r(t))\Delta t}\Delta C$. Let

$$\dot{C}(t) = \frac{dC(t)}{dt}.$$

Since the growth rate of $C$ is

$$\frac{E[\dot{C}(t)]}{C(t)},$$

$E[C(t + \Delta t)]$ can be written as $C(t)e^{\frac{E[\dot{C}(t)]}{C(t)} \cdot \Delta t}$. Thus marginal utility of $E[C(t + \Delta t)]$ is given by:

$$e^{-\rho(t+\Delta t)}E[C(t+\Delta t)] = e^{-\rho(t+\Delta t)}\left\{ C(t)e^{\frac{E[\dot{C}(t)]}{C(t)} \cdot \Delta t} \right\}^{-\varsigma}.$$

The path of consumption to be utility maximizing must satisfy the following equality condition:

$$e^{-\rho t}C(t)^{-\varsigma}\Delta C = e^{-\rho(t+\Delta t)}\left\{ C(t)e^{\frac{E[\dot{C}(t)]}{C(t)} \cdot \Delta t} \right\}^{-\varsigma} e^{E(r(t))\Delta t}\Delta C.$$

Dividing both sides by $e^{-\rho t}C(t)^{-\varsigma}\Delta C$:

$$1 = e^{-\rho\Delta t}\left\{ e^{\frac{E[\dot{C}(t)]}{C(t)} \cdot \Delta t} \right\}^{-\varsigma} e^{E(r(t))\Delta t}.$$

Taking log:

$$-\rho\Delta t - \varsigma\frac{E[\dot{C}(t)]}{C(t)}\Delta t + E[r(t)]\Delta t = 0.$$

Divide by $\Delta t$ and rearranging the terms, the expected growth rate of consumption in country 2 is:

$$\frac{E[\dot{C}_2(t)]}{C_2(t)} = \frac{E[r_2(t)]-\rho}{\varsigma}. \tag{37}$$

### 2.4.4. *Output of the economy*

Substituting the quantity of $E(X_{2j})$ into the production function yields the expected total output of country 2 as:

$$E(Y_2) = (\tilde{A}_2)^{1/(1-\alpha)} \cdot \alpha^{2\alpha/(1-\alpha)} \cdot L_2 \cdot N_2. \tag{38}$$

Thus, expected output per worker in country 2 increases with the expected productivity parameter, $\tilde{A}_2$, and the number of intermediate goods, $N_2$:

$$E(y_2) \equiv \frac{E(Y_2)}{L_2} = (\tilde{A}_2)^{1/(1-\alpha)} \cdot \alpha^{2\alpha/(1-\alpha)} \cdot N_2. \tag{39}$$

### 2.4.5. *Growth rate of $N_2$*

The resources devoted to imitation in country 2 is the savings in each period, which is equal to total output $(Y_2)$, less consumption $(C_2)$, and less quantity of intermediates $N_2 X_2$. The change in $N_2$ denoted as $\Delta N_{2t}$ is given by the resources devoted to imitation divided by the cost of imitation $(v_2)$. Thus:

$$
\begin{aligned}
\Delta N_{2t} &= \frac{1}{v_{2t}} (Y_{2t} - C_{2t} - N_{2t} X_{2t}) \\
&= \frac{1}{v_{2t}} \left[ A_{2t}^{1/(1-\alpha)} \cdot \alpha^{2\alpha/(1-\alpha)} \cdot L_2 N_{2t} - C_{2t} - N_{2t} X_{2t} \right]. \tag{40}
\end{aligned}
$$

It can be seen from equation (40) that change in $N_{2t}$ is an increasing function of $A_{2t}$.

At the beginning of each period, the productivity parameter experiences a stroke of luck, which can be good or bad. In the event of good luck, $\Theta = \Theta^H = 1$:

$$A_{2t}^H = A_{1t} \left( \frac{N_{2t}}{N_{1t}} \right)^\beta$$

$$Y_{2t}^H = (A_{2t}^H)^{1/(1-\alpha)} \alpha^{2\alpha/(1-\alpha)} \cdot L_2 \cdot N_{2t}$$

$$X_{2t}^H = L_2 \cdot (A_{2t}^H)^{1/(1-\alpha)} \alpha^{2/(1-\alpha)}$$

$$C_{2t} = C_{2t}^H$$

$$\Delta N_{2t}^H = \frac{1}{v_{2t}} \left[ (A_{2t}^H)^{1/(1-\alpha)} \cdot \alpha^{2\alpha/(1-\alpha)} \cdot L_2 \cdot N_{2t} - C_{2t}^H - N_{2t} X_{2t}^H \right]$$

$$= \frac{1}{v_{2t}} \left[ (A_{2t}^H)^{1/(1-\alpha)} \cdot L_2 \cdot N_{2t} \cdot (\alpha^{2\alpha/(1-\alpha)} - \alpha^{2/(1-\alpha)}) - C_{2t}^H \right]. \quad (41)$$

In the event of bad luck, $\Theta = \Theta^L < 1$:

$$A_{2t}^L = \Theta^L A_{1t} \left( \frac{N_{2t}}{N_{1t}} \right)^\beta$$

$$Y_{2t}^L = (A_{2t}^L)^{1/(1-\alpha)} \cdot \alpha^{2\alpha/(1-\alpha)} \cdot L_2 \cdot N_{2t}$$

$$X_{2t}^L = L_2 \cdot (A_{2t}^L)^{1/(1-\alpha)} \alpha^{2/(1-\alpha)}$$

$$C_{2t} = C_{2t}^L$$

$$\Delta N_{2t}^L = \frac{1}{v_{2t}} \left[ (A_{2t}^L)^{1/(1-\alpha)} \cdot \alpha^{2\alpha/(1-\alpha)} \cdot L_2 \cdot N_{2t} - C_{2t}^L - N_{2t} X_{2t}^L \right]$$

$$= \frac{1}{v_{2t}} \left[ (A_{2t}^L)^{1/(1-\alpha)} \cdot L_2 \cdot N_{2t} \cdot (\alpha^{2\alpha/(1-\alpha)} - \alpha^{2/(1-\alpha)}) - C_{2t}^L \right]. \quad (42)$$

Comparing equations (41) and (42) and assuming that $C_{2t}^L/Y_{2t}^L = C_{2t}^H/Y_{2t}^H = k$, it can be shown that $\Delta N_{2t}^H > \Delta N_{2t}^L$ for a wide range of values of $k$ and $\alpha$.

The number of intermediate goods in the next period, $N_{2t+1}$, is given by:

$$N_{2t+1} = N_{2t} + \Delta N_{2t} = f(A_{2t}, \Omega). \quad (43)$$

$\Omega$ in equation (43) represents all other variables that affect $N_{2t+1}$. Thus, the luck element affects $\Delta N_2$ and $N_{2t+1}$ through its impact on $A_{2t}$, and $N_{2t+1}$ in turn affects $A_2$ in the period $t+1$. In the event of bad luck, as compared to the event of good luck, the lower $N_2$ in the next period in turn gives rise to lower $A_2$ in the next period.

The growth rate of $N_2$ is given by:

$$\frac{\Delta N_{2t}}{N_{2t}} = \frac{1}{v_{2t}} \left[ (A_{2t})^{1/(1-\alpha)} \cdot L_2 \cdot (\alpha^{2\alpha/(1-\alpha)} - \alpha^{2/(1-\alpha)}) - \frac{C_{2t}}{N_{2t}} \right]. \qquad (44)$$

In the above equation, $N_2/N_1$ has two opposing effects on the growth rate of $N_2$. On the one hand, $A_2$ is positively related to $N_2/N_1$, and thus growth rate of $N_2$ increases as $N_2/N_1$ increases through the effect of $A_2$. On the other hand, the cost of imitation $v_2$ increases as $N_2/N_1$ increases, thus the growth rate of $N_2$ decreases as $N_2/N_1$ increases through the effect of $v_2$. It is postulated that at lower level of output (or $A_2$), the effect of $A_2$ is larger than the effect of $v_2$. At higher level of output (or $A_2$), the effect of $v_2$ is larger than the effect of $A_2$. This is in line with the argument of Phillips and Sul (2003). They suggest that the adoption of technology is slow during the initial phase of development due to lack of infrastructure, which include government policy, software and human capital. Figure 2.1 shows the postulated growth path of $N_2$ as a function of $N_2/N_1$.

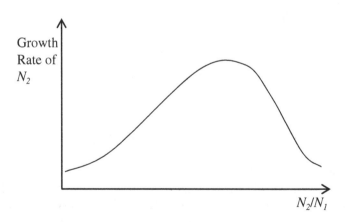

**Fig. 2.1.** Postulated growth path of $N_2$ as a function of $N_2/N_1$.

## 2.4.6. Expected growth rate of $Y_2$

From equations (38) and (39), the expected growth rate of $Y_2$ and $y_2$ are given by:

$$
\begin{aligned}
E\left(\frac{\dot{Y}_{2t}}{Y_{2t}}\right) = E\left(\frac{\dot{y}_{2t}}{y_{2t}}\right) &= \frac{1}{1-\alpha}\cdot\frac{\dot{\tilde{A}}_{2t}}{\tilde{A}_{2t}} + \frac{\dot{N}_{2t}}{N_{2t}} \\
&= \frac{1}{1-\alpha}\left(\frac{\dot{\theta}_t}{\theta_t} + \beta\cdot\frac{\dot{N}_{2t}}{N_{2t}} - \beta\frac{\dot{N}_{1t}}{N_{1t}}\right) + \frac{\dot{N}_{2t}}{N_{2t}} \\
&= \frac{\dot{N}_{2t}}{N_{2t}} + \frac{1}{1-\alpha}\cdot\frac{\dot{\theta}_t}{\theta_t} + \frac{\beta}{1-\alpha}\left(\frac{\dot{N}_{2t}}{N_{2t}} - \frac{\dot{N}_{1t}}{N_{1t}}\right).
\end{aligned}
\tag{45}
$$

The expected growth rate of $Y_2$ is thus a positive function of the growth rate of expansion of intermediate goods $N_2$, the growth rate of the expected probability of having good luck, and the difference in growth rate of $N_2$ and $N_1$.

## 2.4.7. The steady state

In the steady state, $N_2$ grows at the same rate as $Y_2$. According the equation (45), this is achieved when:

$$
\frac{1}{1-\alpha}\cdot\frac{\dot{\theta}_t}{\theta_t} + \frac{\beta}{1-\alpha}\left(\frac{\dot{N}_{2t}}{N_{2t}} - \frac{\dot{N}_{1t}}{N_{1t}}\right) = 0.
\tag{46}
$$

This requires $\dot{\theta}_t/\theta_t = 0$ and $\dot{N}_{2t}/N_{2t} = \dot{N}_{1t}/N_{1t}$. According to the model specification, $p_t \equiv Pr(\Theta_t = \Theta^H) = 1$, and thus $\dot{\theta}_t/\theta_t = 0$ when $A_2$ is sufficiently high.

There are two possible scenarios for $\dot{N}_{2t}/N_{2t} = \dot{N}_{1t}/N_{1t}$ to take place. The first possible steady state occurs at the point where $(N_2/N_1)^* = 1$, such that country 2 copies all available innovations in country 1. In this case, $A_2^*$ is also equal to $A_1$. $N_2$, $Y_2$, and $C_2$ of country 2 will have the same steady state growth rate as country 1. In addition, output per worker and consumption per worker are the same in both countries. Since $A_2^*$ is a constant, profit flow $\pi_2$ and rate of return $r_2$ will also be a constant, such that:

$$r_2^* = \frac{\pi_2}{v_2}. \tag{47}$$

The second possible steady state, where $\dot{N}_{2t}/N_{2t} = \dot{N}_{1t}/N_{1t}$, occurs at a point where the steady state ratio of $N_2/N_1$, $(N_2/N_1)^*$, is a constant but is less than 1. This would occur when the cost of copying increases significantly at higher level of $N_2/N_1$, such that not all innovations in country 1 are copied by country 2. Since $(N_2/N_1)^*$ is a constant that is less than 1, then $A_2^*$ will also be a constant that is less than 1, and the steady state ratio of output per worker $(y_2/y_1)^*$ will be less than 1. Thus the country 2's per worker output would fall short of country 1's per worker output even in the steady state. However, $N_2$, $Y_2$, and $C_2$ of country 2 will still grow at the same steady state growth rate as country 1. Again, as $A_2^*$ is a constant, $r_2^* = \pi_2/v_2$ is a constant.

The above analysis shows that while growth rates converge at the steady state, per capita output level may or may not converge at the steady state depending on the cost of imitation.

### 2.4.8. *Technological leadership*

In the steady state $(N_2/N_1)^* = 1$, there exists a possibility of a switchover in technological leader. Since $C_1$ and $C_2$ grow at the same rate in the long run, if the preference parameters are assumed to be the same in both countries, it would imply that $r_2^* = r_1$. From equations (17) and (47), it would imply that:

$$\frac{\pi_2}{v_2^*} = \frac{\pi_1}{\eta_1}. \tag{48}$$

Substituting in the profit functions, we get:

$$\frac{L_2}{v_2^*} = \frac{L_1}{\eta_1}$$

$$\Rightarrow v_2^* = \frac{L_2}{L_1} \cdot \eta_1. \tag{49}$$

Country 2 will not choose to innovate and will continue to imitate if the cost of imitation at the steady state is lower than the cost of innovation, i.e. $v_2^* < \eta_2$. Conversely, country 2 will choose to innovate and switch over to become the technological leader if $v_2^* > \eta_2$.

From equation (49), country 2 will not innovate if:

$$\eta_2 > \frac{L_2}{L_1} \cdot \eta_1. \tag{50}$$

Country 2 will innovate and country 1 will imitate if:

$$\eta_2 < \frac{L_2}{L_1} \cdot \eta_1. \tag{51}$$

In equations (50) and (51), the size of the population $L$ serves as a scale of complementary domestic inputs. The cost of innovation, together with the scale effect, determines the technological leadership.

## 2.5. Result

The stochastic technological diffusion model with endogenized productivity parameter is able to generate a range of possible outcomes. Some of the outcomes are described as follows:

*Case 1: Turtle Economy that Never Catches Up*

A turtle economy has low $Y_2$ and low $A_2$. Since $p_t \equiv \Pr(\Theta_t = \Theta^H) = g(A_{t-1})$ is small, the tendency for the economy to experience negative shock is high. If the probability of the economy being hit by negative shocks is sufficiently high, the economy is likely to experience short periods of positive growth followed by short periods of negative growth (or growth reversal). The outcome will be a very slow-growing turtle economy that fails to catch-up with the rest of the world.

*Case 2: Turtle Economy that Transforms into a Horse Economy*

A turtle economy that experiences a series of good luck, as represented by $\Theta^H$, will see an improvement in $A_2$. As $A_2$ improves, $p$ also improves. This reduces the probability of experience growth reversal, and allows the economy to continue on its growth path.

*Case 3: Horse Economy that Catches Up with the Elephant Economy*

A horse economy has medium $Y_2$ and medium $A_2$. As $A_2$ improves, the probability of good luck increases. This reduces the tendency of the economy to experience negative shock. The increasing $A_2$ also gives rise to an increasing rate of growth of $N_2$, which in turn gives rise to an increasing rate of growth of $Y_2$. The horse economy grows faster than the elephant economy as the cost of copying is lower than the cost of innovation. The growth rate of $N_2$ (and the growth rate of $Y_2$) eventually slows down as the cost of imitation increases due to the diminishing pool of copiable materials. In the long run, per capita output growth rate converges with that of the elephant economy. Per capita output level may or may not converge with that of the elephant economy depending on the cost of innovations as $N_2/N_1$ increases.

## 2.6. Conclusion

This chapter extends Barro and Sala-i-Martin's (1997) technological diffusion model by endogenizing the productivity parameter and incorporating probability of adverse shocks into the productivity parameter. The functional form that extends the productivity parameter to the technological level (as proxied by $N_2$) encapsulates the idea that social infrastructure, trade and investment openness, and technological advancement are cumulatively correlated. The following insight and policy implications can be drawn from the model:

1.  Developing countries with lower cost of imitation and lower level of consumption will enjoy a higher growth rate of technological diffusion (as proxied by $N_2$) and higher growth rate of output. Thus, government policies that help to lower the cost of technological absorption, such as openness in trade and investment policies, equipping the general population with relevant skills will help spur the growth rate of the nation. Policies that encourage higher level of savings rate will also help to quicken the pace of economic growth.

2.  Although growth rates of the horse economies would approach those of the developed nations in the long run, per capita income levels still may not equalize if the cost of imitation is too high. Deliberate government policies in lowering the cost of imitation would help increase the long-run per capita output level of the developing countries.

3.  Technological leadership among the developed nations is determined by the cost of innovation and the size of the workforce. While the size of the workforce presents a scale effect that is an advantage to the bigger economies, governments' efforts in lower the cost of innovation also play a significant role to promote technological leadership.

4.  Economies at the middle income level (i.e. the horse economies) are less susceptible to negative shocks and are able to achieve quantum leap in technological advances as a result of technological diffusion. On the other hand, economies with low income levels (i.e. the turtle economies) are constantly challenged by negative shocks and are more likely to encounter growth reversal. As a result, income levels of the horse economies could converge towards those of the elephant economies, while income levels of the turtle economies would diverge away from the rest of the world. This model predicts that in the long run there will be convergence at the upper-income levels of the world economy but overall divergence of the world economy.

5. Negative shock to the productivity parameter is one of the main causes of slow growth of the poor developing countries. Although the model has described the occurrence of negative shocks as purely by chance, it does not diminish the importance of good social infrastructure (or good governance) in economic development. World institutions that are involved in poverty alleviation should focus on reducing the "negative shocks" by strengthening the governance in the poor developing countries.

## CHAPTER 3

# Testing of Growth Convergence and Economic Transition Under the Framework of the S-Curve Hypothesis

## 3.1. Introduction

### 3.1.1. *S-Curve hypothesis' predictions on growth convergence*

The S-Curve hypothesis (Lim, 1994, 1996, 2009) classifies the world economies into three broad groups according to their income levels and growth rates: turtle economies with low income levels and low growth rates, horse economies with middle income levels and high growth rates and elephant economies with high income levels but low growth rates. With economies growing at two different bands of growth rates, the S-Curve hypothesis thus suggests the co-existence of the dichotomy between convergence and divergence in the world economy. The faster-growing horse economies will converge towards the elephant economies at the upper tier of the world economy, while the turtle economies will divergence further and further away from the rest of the world.

According to the S-Curve hypothesis, the superlative growth rates of the horse economies are due to high investment rates and quantum leaps in technological level (Lim, 2005). The improving social infrastructure of the horse economies helps attract domestic and foreign investments, while the relatively low level of development of the horse economies enables the quantum-leap transfer of technology, organizational skills and production techniques from the developed nations. On the other hand, the investment rates in the developed nations are likely to be low due to diminishing marginal returns, and the scope of quantum-leap transfer of technology among the developed countries is likely to be very limited. The growth rate of the developed countries would then depend mainly on the rate of technological progress of the global economy. As a result of the faster pace of growth, the income levels of the horse economies will converge to those of the elephant economies. Along the same line of argument, the S-Curve hypothesis also implies that no country can continue to grow superlatively forever. The phase of rapid growth would eventually come to an end when the technological gap between the horse economies and the developed countries closes and quantum-leap transfer of technology is no longer possible.

There is no "automatic" internal mechanism within the S-Curve hypothesis that would lift a turtle economy out of the doldrums and onto a path of rapid development. The S-Curve hypothesis takes the view that unless there is a significant elevation of the EGOIN of a country, in particular $G$, a turtle economy would not be able to transform into a horse economy and would remain poor. In other words, the S-Curve hypothesis does not support the view of ultimate convergence, where all poor countries, in a matter of time, will become rich eventually.

The S-Curve hypothesis thus has the following 3 predictions on growth convergence:

1.  Income levels of horse economies to converge to those of the elephant economies, and growth rates of horse economies to eventually slow down as their income levels approach those of the elephant economies;
2.  Growth divergence would take place at the bottom end of the world income spectrum as not all turtle economies would advance to become horse economies;
3.  Convergence and divergence would take place simultaneously in the world economy, and there will be no ultimate convergence.

The S-Curve hypothesis, however, does not describe the probable growth paths of economies undergoing transition. While a horse economy could converge monotonically to the income level of the developed nations, the S-Curve hypothesis does not rule out the possibility of transitional divergence but eventual convergence. Similarly, a turtle economy could undergo transitional convergence but eventually diverge away from the global economy. It would be a fruitful exercise to empirically determine the transition paths of the horse and the turtle economies. This would also enhance our understanding of the pattern and the speed of convergence of the developing countries.

### 3.1.2.  *Econometric modeling of growth convergence by Phillips and Sul*

Based on the empirical support of long-term growth patterns, Phillips and Sul (2003, 2005) take the view that the world economy is undergoing transient divergence but will achieve ultimate convergence. Although the authors state that they do not expect all countries to converge as empirical distribution of growth and per capita income level will always exist, they feel that there can be convergence in the sense of "an elimination of divergent behavior (even as the poorest countries begin to catch up) and an ultimate narrowing of the differences". In fact, they make repeated reference to the recent theoretical model by Lucas (2002, 2004) that suggests transient divergence but ultimate convergence in the global economy.

The work by Lucas will be briefly discussed here as it was mentioned several times in Phillips and Sul's papers and is believed to have influenced the research of Phillips and Sul. Lucas' (2002, 2004) theoretical framework attempts to explain the stagnant growth rate of per capita income of the world economy before 1800 and the accelerating income growth thereafter. Lucas attributes the per capita income growth after 1800 to the Industrial Revolution and the associated demographic transition. Demographic transition refers to the reduction in population growth rates, after initial increase, as per capita incomes continue to increase. Demographic transition took place as parents chose to increase the quality rather than the quantity of children as returns to human capital increased, and returns to human capital increased as a result of industrialization. More notably, these increases in returns to human capital generate important stimulating effects. It stimulated parents to opt for smaller family size. In addition, it stimulated other families to accumulate human capital. It also stimulated people across national borders to accumulate human capital. However, as the Industrial Revolution did not affect all parts of the world uniformly, income inequality worsened sharply since the beginning of the Industrial Revolution. This explains the current growth divergence. Nevertheless, Lucas predicts ultimate convergence. He suggests that as the newly industrializing economies catch up with the income levels of the wealthiest countries, their growth rates of both population and income will slow down to rates that are close to the wealthiest countries. "At the same time, countries that have been kept out of this process of diffusion by socialist planning or simply by corruption and lawlessness will, one after another, join the Industrial Revolution and become the miracle economies of the future." In his view, the most important factor that will accelerate the process of catching up for the backward economies is "dealing on a day-to-day basis with more advance economies", and in particular, trade.

Phillips and Sul's (2003, 2005) objectives are to model economic transitions and to test growth convergence econometrically. Specifically, they want to devise an econometric testing method that allows for transient divergence but ultimate convergence of the world economy. The authors disagree with the assumptions of homogeneity in technological progress and homogeneity in the speed of convergence over time and across countries that are conveniently but erroneously used in many other empirical studies on growth convergence. They argue that the assumption of homogeneity in technological progress is only appropriate for countries that are in or near steady state. When this assumption is forced upon transitional economies, the test could conclude an absence of convergence when in fact it is only transitional divergence. In these studies, very often the only source of heterogeneity across countries stems from the initial conditions of these countries. As a result, Phillips and Sul feel that the hypothesis tests of these studies do not necessarily imply growth convergence or divergence. They argue that permitting for heterogeneity in technological progress and heterogeneity in speed of convergence would allow for the case of transient divergence but ultimate convergence of the world economy.

Phillips and Sul (2003, 2005) extend the neoclassical growth models to allow for heterogeneity in the growth rate of technological progress across countries and over time. Similar to Lim's (1994, 1996, 2009) S-Curve hypothesis, quantum-leap in technology transfer is also quoted by Phillips and Sul as the chief explanation of faster growth rate. By assuming that different countries utilize technological progress to varying extents at different times, various time paths of transitional divergence and convergence of these countries can be derived. It is useful to note that Phillips and Sul choose to focus on relative economic growth rather than economic growth. Economic growth is measured relatively to the average performance in a subgroup of economies or an individual benchmark like that of the US economy. The degree of departure from the subgroup average or the benchmark is captured by the *transitional parameter*. When fitted with observable data on per capita real income, the time path of the transition parameter of individual economies, which is termed as relative transition curve, can reveal the empirical properties of these economies in transition. In addition, Phillips and Sul also developed a regression test of the hypothesis of convergence that is based on the variance estimate of the transition parameter.

### 3.1.3. *Synergizing Lim's S-Curve hypothesis and Phillips and Sul's modeling of economic transition*

Lim (1996) developed the S-Curve hypothesis to describe the general development path of economies; Phillips and Sul (2003, 2005) developed the economic transition parameter and the associated variance ratio test to shed light on the growth paths of economies and to test for economic convergence. While Lim's theory is highly qualitative, Phillips and Sul's work is thoroughly quantitative. Although the objectives and the approaches of Lim, and Phillips and Sul are very different, both works are highly complementary.

There is however one key difference in the theoretical framework of Lim and that of Phillips and Sul, although it does not affect the empirical applicability of Phillips and Sul's methodology on the S-Curve hypothesis. Lim takes the view that unless there is a significant elevation of the EGOIN of a country, in particular G, a turtle economy would not be able to transform into a horse economy and would remain poor. Phillips and Sul, on the other hand, take the view that development will occur in a matter of time — a "poorest economy" would grow very slowly, but would eventually become a "poor economy", and then a "middle-income economy", and then a "rich economy", and finally a "richest economy"; and as it develops, its growth will also gain momentum.[1] In the theoretical framework of Phillips and Sul, there is transitional divergence but ultimate convergence, whilst there is no ultimate convergence in the S-Curve hypothesis.

In the following sections, Phillips and Sul's transition parameter and transition curve will be employed to shed light on the empirical properties of the growth path of economies at different stages of development: turtle, horse and elephant. Phillips and Sul's variance ratio test will also be used to test for economic convergence under the framework of the S-Curve hypothesis.

---

[1] See Figure 1.5 for a graphical illustration.

The outline of this chapter is as follows: The economic transition curve and the associated variance ratio test of growth convergence developed by Phillips and Sul will be reviewed in Section 3.2. The relative transition paths of the turtle, horse and elephant economies are plotted and analyzed in Section 3.3 to shed light on the empirical properties of the growth path of economies at different stages of development. The econometric testing of growth convergence can be found in Section 3.4. A conclusion is given in the last section.

## 3.2. Review of Phillips and Sul's Methodology

### 3.2.1. *Modeling economic transitions*

Phillips and Sul (2003, 2005) begin with the basic neoclassical growth model. Based on the production function with labor-augmented technological progress and assuming a Cobb–Douglas technology, the transitional growth path for country $i$ at time period $t$ is given as:

$$\log y_{it} = \log \tilde{y}_i^* + [\log \tilde{y}_{i0} - \log \tilde{y}_i^*]e^{-\beta_{it}t} + \log A_{it}, \qquad (1)$$

where $y_i$ is per capita real income;

$\tilde{y}_i = \frac{y_i}{A_i}$ is real income per effective labor unit;

$A_i$ is the state of technology;
$\tilde{y}_i^*$ is steady state real income per effective labor unit;
$\beta_i$ is the speed of convergence parameter[2];

Technological progress is assumed to follow a simple exponential path $A_{it} = A_{i0}e^{x_{it}t}$, where $x_{it}$ is growth rate of technological progress. Phillips and Sul allow $x_{it}$ to change over time and across countries. This is a significant improvement over the very restrictive assumption of homogeneity of $x_{it}$ used in other empirical studies.

---

[2] As usual, the speed of convergence is negatively related to the technology parameter $\alpha_i$ in the Cobb–Douglas production function, and positively related to the rate of depreciation, the growth rate of population and the growth rate of technological progress.

Since $\log A_{it} = \log A_{i0} + x_{it}t$, Equation (1) can be rewritten as:

$$\log y_{it} = \log \tilde{y}_i^* + \log A_{i0} + [\log \tilde{y}_{i0} - \log \tilde{y}_i^*]e^{-\beta_{it}t} + x_{it}t$$
$$= a_{it} + x_{it}t \qquad (2)$$

where $a_{it} = \log \tilde{y}_i^* + \log A_{i0} + [\log \tilde{y}_{i0} - \log \tilde{y}_i^*]e^{-\beta_{it}t}$.

Phillips and Sul (2005) theorize that although technology is a public good that is widely available. The ability to utilize the common technology differs across countries, and thus growth rates of technological progress are heterogeneous across countries. Developed countries are the creators of new technology. They are able to incorporate the full extent of the present level of technology into their production process. Thus, growth rate of technological progress in the developed nations is the same as the speed of technological creation. Developing countries are the followers. They have to go through the process of learning the earlier technology first and they also have to develop the necessary infrastructure gradually to absorb and utilize the technology. Thus, the rate of technological progress in the developing countries is determined by the speed of technological learning, or technological transfer. The speed of technological learning can be faster or slower than the speed of technological creation. When an economy is very poor and lacks the necessary infrastructure and human capital, the speed of technological learning in the poor economy tends to be lower than the speed of technological creation in the rich economy. Divergence is therefore likely to occur. As the speed of learning gradually picks up, the speed of learning could even outpace the speed of technological creation, and thus enable the poor economy to catch up with its richer counterpart.

In the econometric model, all economies are assumed to share a common growth component, such as technology; although different economies utilize the common growth component to varying extents. The common growth component is represented by $\mu_t$. From equation (2), we have:

$$\log y_{it} = \left(\frac{a_{it} + x_{it}t}{\mu_t}\right)\mu_t = b_{it}\mu_t \qquad (3)$$

where $b_{it}$ measures the share of the common component $\mu_t$ that economy $i$ experiences. During the transitional period, $b_{it}$ is a function of the speed of convergence $\beta_i$, the growth rate of technological progress $x_i$, and the initial growth component level $y_{i0}$. Figure 3.1 shows the possible transition paths for three types of economies as they approach the common growth path.

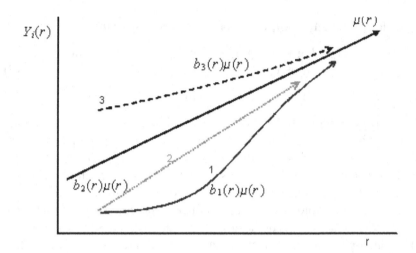

**Fig. 3.1.**    Possible transition paths.

*Source*: Phillips and Sul (2005).

Economies 1 and 2 are poor countries initially while economy 3 is a rich economy with a higher initial income. Economy 2, representing those newly industrializing and fast-growing economies such as Singapore and China, has higher $\beta$ than economy 3. This enables economy 2 to catch up with economy 3, i.e. $\beta$-convergence holds in this case. Economy 1 has the lowest $\beta$. Economy 1 has similar initial endowment as economy 2, but this country's growth diverges from economies 2 and 3 initially. This is a case of transient divergence but ultimate convergence.

Supposing $\log y_{it}$ is observable and $\log y_{it} = b_{it}\mu_t$ holds, the standardized quantity can be obtained by taking ratios to cross-sectional averages:

$$h_{itN} = \frac{\log y_{it}}{\frac{1}{N}\sum_{i=1}^{N}\log y_{it}} = \frac{b_{it}}{\frac{1}{N}\sum_{i=1}^{N}b_{it}} \tag{4}$$

If growth convergences, then:

$$\lim_{t\to\infty} b_{it} = b \quad \text{and} \quad \lim_{t\to\infty}\frac{1}{N}\sum_{i=1}^{N}b_{it} = b$$

so that $\lim_{t\to\infty} h_{itN} = 1$

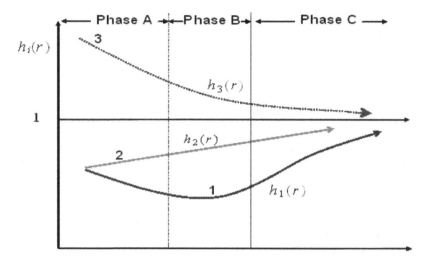

**Fig. 3.2.**   Relative transition curves.

*Source*: Phillips and Sul (2005).

$h_{itN}$ is known as the "*transition parameter*", and can be regarded as the degree of departure from the steady state. Its behavior as $t \to \infty$ reflects convergence of $b_{it}$.

The time path $h_{itN}$ sketches the *relative transition curve* of the economy. Figure 3.2 shows the possible patterns of the relative transition curve, each satisfying the growth convergence condition of $\lim_{t \to \infty} h_{itN} = 1$. Economies 2 and 3, representing the newly industrializing economies and the rich developed economies respectively, converge monotonically to unite on two different transition paths. Economy 1, on the other hand, has the same starting per capita income level as Economy 2 but its relative transition path involves an initial phase of divergence from the group, followed by a catch-up period, and converges later.

### 3.2.2. *Testing convergence using variance ratio*

Phillips and Sul then proceed to develop a regression test of the hypothesis of convergence that is based on the variance estimate of the transition parameter. For a subgroup $G$ of $N_G$ economies, variance estimate for $h_{it}^G$ can be calculated from:

$$H_t^{\,G} = \sigma_G^2 = \frac{1}{N_G}\sum_{i=1}^{N_G}(h_{it}^G - 1)^2 \tag{5}$$

Assuming the sample variance of the relative transition follows a decay model that has the parametric form $H_t^G \sim (A/t^{2\alpha})$ in the limit as $t \to \infty$, the logarithm of $H_t^G$ can be written in the form of a regression model:

$$\log H_t^G = \log A - 2\alpha \log t + u_t^G \tag{6}$$

The error term, $u_t^G$, is shown in Phillips and Sul (2005) to be asymptotically equivalent to a zero mean, weakly dependent time series.

The regression of equation (6) is then used as a test of the hypothesis of convergence. Specifically, when $\alpha > 0$, $\log H_t^G$ and hence $H_t^G$ decreases with $t$, implying convergence in subgroup $G$. Conversely, when $\alpha = 0$, $\log H_t^G$ and hence $H_t^G$ does not converge to zero. Thus there is no convergence in the subgroup $G$.

The hypothesis testing is as follows:

Test    $H_0$: $\alpha = 0$

    $H_1$: $\alpha > 0$

Rejecting $H_0$ provides empirical evidence in favor of convergence among the economies in subgroup $G$ and the value of $\alpha$ is a measure of the rate of convergence.

Phillips and Sul point out that it is difficult and less meaningful to test for growth convergence for short-time series, as transitions are generally still occurring because of temporal heterogeneity in key parameters. However, even in such cases, the fitted transition curve may still reveal interesting empirical properties of the individual economies in transition.

### 3.3. Analysis of Transition Paths

#### 3.3.1. *Data and categorization of economies*

The data series used in this paper is real GDP per capita (Laspeyres) from Penn World Table 6.1 from 1950 to 2000 (Heston, Summers and Aten,

2002). This data series is both PPP-adjusted and inflation-adjusted with 1996 as the base year. Although data on 168 countries are available from the PWT 6.1, only 115 countries with GDP per capita data spanning across more than 30 years are used in the following analysis.

*Categorization of economies*

These 115 countries are categorized into turtle, horse and elephant economies based on their per capita GDP level and long-run per capita growth rate. The graphical plot of the long-run GDP per capita growth rate (1961–2000) against per capita GDP level in 1990 is shown in Fig. 3.3. The cluster on the leftmost is the turtle economies; these countries have low income levels and low or even negative growth rates. The cluster in the center with significantly higher growth rate is the horse economies. The cluster on the rightmost with high income level but growth rate of not more than 4% is the elephant economies. There are a handful of economies that could not be neatly placed into the three categories. The

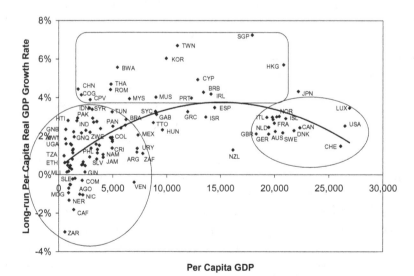

**Fig. 3.3.** Average annual GDP per capita growth rate from 1961–2000 versus GDP per capita in 1990 (international $ in 1996 prices).

*Source*: Computed from data from PWT 6.1 (Heston *et al.*, 2002).

list of these economies and their abbreviations can be found in the Appendix.

There are 16 horse economies in Fig. 3.3: China, Republic of Congo, Cape Verde, Romania, Thailand and Botswana are the early horses; in the middle are Malaysia, Mauritius, South Korea, Taiwan, Portugal, Cyprus, Barbados and Ireland; Singapore and Hong Kong are at the tail-end of the phase of horse economy. Among the 16 countries, the Republic of Congo, an economy that reaps its fortune from its oil reserve, is most at risk of slipping back to a turtle economy as a result of its government budget problems and the ethnic unrest in the country.

There are a total of 17 elephant economies in the rightmost cluster: Luxembourg, United States, Switzerland, Canada, Denmark, Iceland, Sweden, Norway, Finland, Australia, France, Belgium, Italy, Austria, Netherlands, United Kingdom and Germany. All these countries have GDP per capita of more than 18,000 International Dollars in 1990 (measured in 1996 prices), and GDP per capita growth rate of less than 4% between 1961–2000. Japan, although not included in the cluster as it has an average annual growth rate of 4.3%, is rightly an elephant economy. The high annual growth rate between 1961–2000 is due to the 6.3% average annual growth rate achieved between 1961–1980; its average annual growth rate in the last two decades is 2.3% and its average annual growth rate in the last decade is only 1.1%. The Japanese economy has slowed down significantly, as it transforms from a horse economy to an elephant economy.

There are a handful of economies that could not be neatly placed into the three categories: Trinidad & Tobago, Gabon, Seychelles, Hungary, Greece, Israel, Spain and New Zealand. These 8 countries have relatively low growth rates as compared to their counterparts of similar income levels. Some of these countries, such as New Zealand, Spain, Israel and Greece could be "Economy 3" as illustrated in Fig. 1.2 in Chapter 1. These countries could be considered as elephant economies, but their per capita GDP levels are lower than other elephant economies due to constraints such as geographical location, political state of affairs, lack of natural resources and even cultural and social norms. In the case of New Zealand, the real per capita income may be understated by the imperfection of GDP that ignores factors such as clean air and good environment.

The rest of the countries are the turtle economies and they represent more than 63% of the total number of countries in this sample. This percentage will be higher in the global population as many turtle economies are not included in this exercise due to insufficient data points. Most of the turtle economies are from Africa and America. In Southeast Asia, Indonesia and the Philippines are classified as the turtle economies.

*Fitting the transition curve*

Although the value of log $y_{it}$, where $y_{it}$ is the per capita GDP of country $i$ at time $t$ is available directly from PWT6.1, we follow the recommendation of Phillips and Sul to remove the business cycle components from the data so as to reveal the long-run trend component. Phillips and Sul suggested using smoothing methods such as the Whittaker–Hodrick–Prescott (WHP) smoothing filter, which has the advantages of being flexible, only requiring the input of a smoothing parameter, and does not require prior specification of the nature of the common trend. In addition, the method is also suitable when the time series is short.

The Hodrick–Prescott filter from Eview5 is used to remove the business cycle components from log $y_{it}$ of the 115 countries. The chosen smoothing parameter is $\lambda = 100$. Using the trend estimate $\hat{f}_{it}$ from the smoothing filter, the estimates for the transition parameter $\hat{h}_{it} = \hat{f}_{it} \big/ \frac{1}{N}\sum_{i=1}^{N}\hat{f}_{it}$ can thus be obtained.

### 3.3.2. *Relative transition curves of the 3 groups of economies*

Figure 3.4 plots the time path of the transition parameters (also known as relative transition curve) of the three categories of economies from 1960 to 1996. It can be seen from Fig. 3.4 that although the turtle economies and the horse economies started at about the same level in 1960, the fortunes of these two groups of economies were very different. While the horse economies were catching up steadily with the elephant economies, the turtle economies diverged further and further away from the rest of the world. Overall, there is no sign of convergence of the world economy.

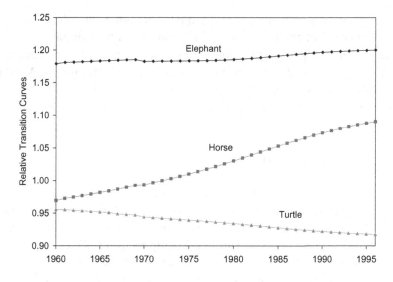

**Fig. 3.4.**   Transition paths of the 3 groups of economies.

### 3.3.3. *Relative transition curves of the elephant economies*

Figure 3.5 plots the relative transition curve of the 18 elephant economies from 1950–2000. It is evident from the diagram that there is a marked reduction in dispersion of the relative transition curves over the period. In addition, there is a narrowing in the relative transition curves towards unity, indicating a tendency to converge towards the end of the period.

There are three observations that stand out in Fig. 3.5. Firstly, Luxembourg is clearly diverging from the rest of the elephant economies since early 1980 on the back of its impressive and sustained growth rate. Luxembourg is a small country with a population of less than 500,000 people; its ability to sustain high growth rate despite having the highest per capita GDP level in the world sets itself as an interesting role model for Singapore. The success of Luxembourg could be attributed to the following factors: close proximity to France, Belgium, and Germany, openness to foreign and cross-border workers which accounts for more than 30% of labor force, a diversified industrial base, and a flourishing financial sector.

Secondly, although USA appears to converge towards the rest of the elephant economies, its transition parameter was consistently higher than

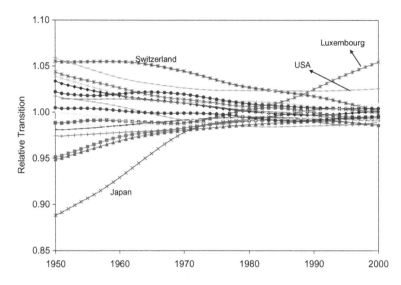

**Fig. 3.5.** Transition paths of elephant economies.

the other elephant economies (with the exception of Switzerland and Luxembourg). In other words, although the growth rates of USA may have converged towards those of other elephant economies, its income level in long-run equilibrium remains higher than those of other elephant economies. Economies of scale could be a possible explanation of its sustained higher income level. Other possible explanations include openness to foreign workers, higher degree of flexibility in its labor market, high level of entrepreneurship, and its attractiveness as a destination for foreign investment.

Thirdly, Japan, which started at a significantly lower per capita GDP level in 1950, had converged very rapidly towards the rest of the elephant economies. The performance of the Japanese economy between 1950 and 1970 resembled that of a horse economy; it gradually transformed into a full-fledge elephant economy onwards from the 1970s.

### 3.3.4. *Relative transition curves of the horse economies*

Figure 3.6 plots the relative transition curve of the 16 horse economies from 1950–2000. As the starting points and the transition paths of the

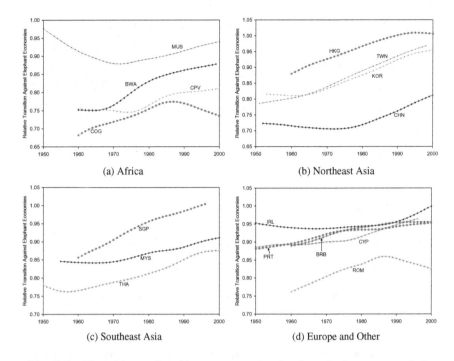

**Fig. 3.6.**    Transition paths of horse economies (against elephant economies).

16 economies vary greatly, the plot of the relative transition curves is separated into four figures categorized according to their geographical region
for better visual clarity. The transition parameters are computed against
the benchmark of the elephant economies. Thus, countries with transition
parameters approaching "one" are countries whose per capita GDP levels
are converging towards that of the elephant economies.

With the exception of Republic of Congo (COG in (a)) and Romania
(ROM in (d)), all other horse economies are converging towards the
income level of the elephant economies. The transition parameters of
Singapore, Hong Kong and Ireland were "one" or exceeded "one" by
2000. In other words, these three countries' per capita GDP levels are on
par with those of the elephant economies. It is also evident from Fig. 3.6
that the speeds of convergence vary greatly even among the horse
economies. Thus it may not be meaningful to talk about a "common" rate
of convergence for the horse economies in general.

The Republic of Congo and Romania are examples of horse economies that suffered a U-turn in their growth path. Among the two, the Republic of Congo, an economy which reaps its fortune from its oil reserve, is more at risk of slipping back to a turtle economy as a result of its government budget problems and the ethnic unrest in the country. Romania, on the other hand, experienced a decade of economic instability and decline after the Communist regime was overthrown in late 1989, led in part by an obsolete industrial base and a lack of structural reform. However, the economic outlook of Romania improved significantly since 2000 onwards, and could be back on track as that of a horse economy.

### 3.3.5. *Relative transition curves of the turtle economies*

Figure 3.7 plots the relative transition curve of the 73 horse economies from 1950–2000. Again, in an attempt to improve the visual clarity of the diagram, the plot of the relative transition curves is separated into 13 graphical plots categorized according to their geographical region. The transition parameters are measured against the benchmark of the elephant economies.

In sharp contrast with the upward trending relative transition curves of the horse economies, the relative transition curves of the turtle economies are mostly downward trending, indicating that they are diverging further and further away from the developed economies. Several other countries have flat relative transition curves. All these countries can be characterized as "economy 1" in the "Phase A" of development as illustrated in Fig. 3.2. There are a handful of countries that exhibited the Phase B turn-around as illustrated in Fig. 3.2; they are Uganda (UGA), Egypt (EGY), Chile (CHL) and India (IND). If these countries continue with their growth momentum, they could eventually transform into a horse economy. Tunisia (TUN) stands out as the only country that is consistently catching up, albeit very slowly, with the developed nations.

### 3.4. Econometric Testing of Growth Convergence

The log $t$ regression test based on equation (6) is conducted with the PWT data set with 115 economies. The result is shown in Table 3.1. With the

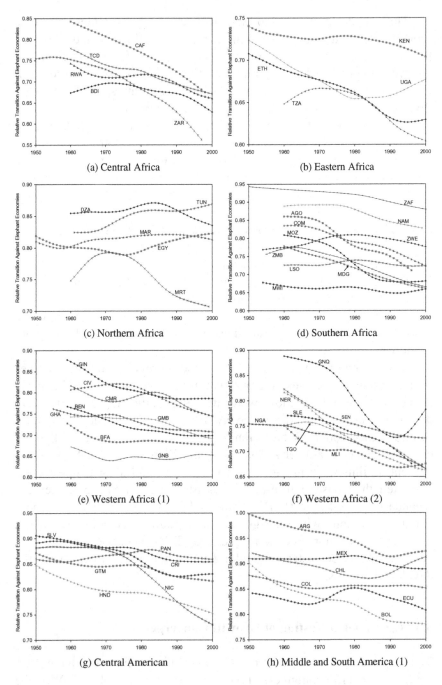

**Fig. 3.7.**   Transition paths of turtle economies (against elephant economies).

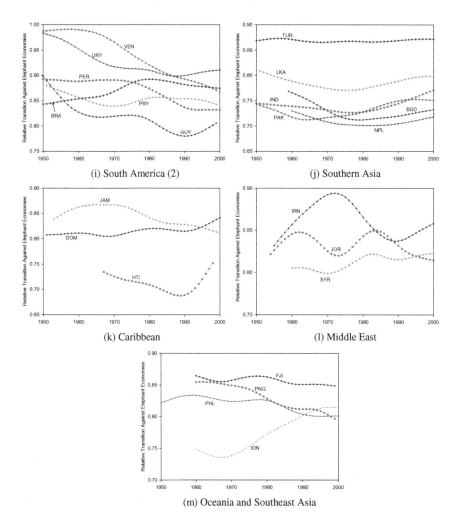

**Fig. 3.7.** (*Continued.*)

full-group test, $\alpha$ is negative and significant, thus we cannot reject the null hypothesis of no convergence among the 115 economies.[3]

Additional tests are then conducted on the three subgroups: elephant, horse and turtle. The results as given in Table 3.1 show that the null

---

[3] Phillips and Sul (2005) point out that the log $t$ test may not perform well in terms of the accuracy of its nominal size when there are a large number of heterogeneous cross-sectional units. Simulation tests show a tendency to over-reject the null hypothesis in such situations.

**Table 3.1.**  Econometric testing of growth convergence.

| Regression: $\log H_t^G = \log A - 2\alpha \log t + u_t^G$ | | |
|---|---|---|
| **Cases** | $\hat{\alpha}$ | *t* **ratio** |
| *log t test within panel* | | |
| All 115 economies | −0.091 | −15.52 |
| *Subgroup log t test for 115 economies* | | |
| 18 elephant economies | 0.460 | 15.16 |
| 16 horse economies | 0.020 | 2.39 |
| 73 turtle economies | −0.044 | −7.33 |
| *Subgroup log t test for 73 turtle economies* | | |
| 39 African turtle economies | −0.017 | −2.30 |
| 34 Other turtle economies | 0.024 | 2.34 |

*Source*: Penn World Table 6.1 (Heston *et al.*, 2002).
*Note*: Sample period is from 1950 to 2000.

hypothesis is rejected for the elephant economies and horse economies at the 5% level; the results imply subgroup convergence. However, the null hypothesis cannot be rejected for the turtle economies, and this implies that there is no subgroup convergence even within the turtle economies.

We further divide the 73 turtle economies into 39 African turtle economies and 34 turtle economies from other regions. The results are given in Table 3.1. The results show that while there is evidence of subgroup convergence among the turtle economies from regions outside Africa, there is no subgroup convergence within the turtle economies in Africa. The consistent under-performance of the African countries is well-recorded in the literature and is termed as the "African dummy". Researchers such as Barro (1991), Mauro (1995), Easterly and Levine (1997), and Temple and Johnson (1998) have shown that despite controlling for variables such as level of investments, government consumption, school enrollment, political stability, corruption, red tape, quality of judiciary and ethnic heterogeneity, the "African dummy" in various empirical growth models was found to be significant and negatively associated with growth. The Triple C theory, also by Lim (1996, 2005), postulates that economic growth is propelled by three engines: the domestic, the regional and the global. In the case of Africa, the very weak regional engine may have hurt the growth prospects of all the African economies in general.

## 3.5. Conclusion

The following conclusions can be drawn from the relative transition curves and the variance ratio econometric tests:

1. There is no overall convergence of the world economy. While this is insufficient to deduce that there is no ultimate convergence of the world economy, there is evidence that the poorest countries (especially those in the African region) are not catching up with the rest of the world in the last 40–50 years.
2. While convergence exists among the elephant economies, countries such as Luxembourg and the United States that have a higher degree of openness to foreign workers and foreign capital outperform other developed nations in terms of income level and growth rate.
3. The horse economies are catching up steadily with the elephant economies, but their speeds of convergence vary widely. Thus it may not be meaningful to talk about a "common" rate of convergence for the horse economies in general.
4. The Republic of Congo and Romania are examples of horse economies that suffered a U-turn in their growth path. If the regression continues, these countries are at risk of slipping back to become turtle economies.
5. The turtle economies are diverging from the elephant economies. Only a handful of turtle economies, such as Uganda, Egypt, Chile and India, exhibited economic turn-around, and these countries are potential horse economies in the future.
6. There is no subgroup convergence among the African turtle economies. The very weak regional engine of Africa may have hurt the growth prospects of most of the African economies.

## 3.6. Appendix: List of Economies and Their Abbreviations

| Elephant economy | | |
| --- | --- | --- |
| Australia (AUS) | Finland (FIN) | Japan (JPN) |
| Austria (AUT) | France (FRA) | Luxembourg (LUX) |
| Belgium (BEL) | United Kingdom (GBR) | Netherlands (NLD) |
| Canada (CAN) | Germany (GER) | Norway (NOR) |
| Switzerland (CHE) | Iceland (ISL) | Sweden (SWE) |
| Denmark (DNK) | Italy (ITA) | United States (USA) |

| Horse economy | | |
| --- | --- | --- |
| Barbados (BRB) | Hong Kong (HKG) | Portugal (PRT) |
| Botswana (BWA) | Ireland (IRL) | Romania (ROM) |
| China (CHN) | Korea, Republic of (KOR) | Singapore (SGP) |
| Congo, Republic of (COG) | Mauritius (MUS) | Thailand (THA) |
| Cape Verde (CPV) | Malaysia (MYS) | Taiwan (TWN) |
| Cyprus (CYP) | | |

| Turtle economy | | |
| --- | --- | --- |
| Angola (AGO) | Equatorial Guinea (GNQ) | Nepal (NPL) |
| Argentina (ARG) | Guatemala (GTM) | Pakistan (PAK) |
| Burundi (BDI) | Guyana (GUY) | Panama (PAN) |
| Benin (BEN) | Honduras (HND) | Peru (PER) |
| Burkina Faso (BFA) | Haiti (HTI) | Philippines (PHL) |
| Bangladesh (BGD) | Indonesia (IDN) | Papua New Guinea (PNG) |
| Bolivia (BOL) | India (IND) | Paraguay (PRY) |
| Brazil (BRA) | Iran (IRN) | Rwanda (RWA) |
| Central African Republic (CAF) | Jamaica (JAM) | Senegal (SEN) |
| Chile (CHL) | Jordan (JOR) | Sierra Leone (SLE) |
| Cote d'Ivoire (CIV) | Kenya (KEN) | El Salvador (SLV) |
| Cameroon (CMR) | Sri Lanka (LKA) | Syria (SYR) |
| Colombia (COL) | Lesotho (LSO) | Chad (TCD) |

*(Continued.)*

## (*Continued.*)

| Turtle economy | | |
|---|---|---|
| Comoros (COM) | Morocco (MAR) | Togo (TGO) |
| Costa Rica (CRI) | Madagascar (MDG) | Tunisia (TUN) |
| Dominican Republic (DOM) | Mexico (MEX) | Turkey (TUR) |
| Algeria (DZA) | Mali (MLI) | Tanzania (TZA) |
| Ecuador (ECU) | Mozambique (MOZ) | Uganda (UGA) |
| Egypt (EGY) | Mauritania (MRT) | Uruguay (URY) |
| Ethiopia (ETH) | Malawi (MWI) | Venezuela (VEN) |
| Fiji (FJI) | Namibia (NAM) | South Africa (ZAF) |
| Ghana (GHA) | Niger (NER) | Congo, Dem. Rep. (ZAR) |
| Guinea (GIN) | Nigeria (NGA) | Zambia (ZMB) |
| Gambia, The (GMB) | Nicaragua (NIC) | Zimbabwe (ZWE) |
| Guinea-Bissau (GNB) | | |

# CHAPTER 4

# Hypothesis of the S-Curve of Capital Accumulation and Its Implied Capital-Output Ratios

## 4.1. Introduction

According to Lim's S-Curve hypothesis (1994, 1996, 2009), the development of an economy can be divided into three stages: (1) low per capita income and low growth rate; (2) middle per capita income and high growth rate; and (3) high per capita income and low growth rate. The S-Curve hypothesis attributes the superlative growth rates of the Stage 2 economies to two important drivers: rapid accumulation of physical capital and quantum-leap improvement in technological capability as a result of technological transfer.

   This chapter turns the spotlight onto one of the two drivers behind the superlative growth: capital accumulation. How important is capital accumulation in generating output growth? Is growth of physical capital the cause or the result of output growth? Proponents of capital fundamentalism such as Arthur Lewis and Walt Rostow have argued that capital formation is an important determinant of economic growth. In their view, increase in savings and increase in investment are critical conditions for economic take-off. De Long and Summers (1991, 1992, 1993) show that investment in machinery and equipment has a strong association with growth, and the association remains strong for the developing countries. They thus advocate a policy bias in favor of equipment investment. More recently, an empirical study by Hill and Hill (2005) using panel data of 100 countries also found that investment share of real GDP is always significant and explains a substantial proportion of real per capita GDP growth.

Statistical evidence has shown that capital accumulation is strongly associated with output growth; however, association is different from causality. Results from the empirical studies on causality are mixed, although studies using panel data often produce results that disagree with the theory of capital fundamentalism. On the other hand, studies on individual countries show that the causal relationship between investment and growth is country-specific and may run in either direction. Blomstrom, Lipsey and Zejan (1996) divide the post-WWII period into five-year sub-periods, and find that per capita GDP growth in a period is more closely related to the subsequent ratio of fixed capital formation to GDP than to the current or past ratio. Their tests on causality also suggest that growth causes subsequent capital formation more than capital formation causes growth. Podrecca and Carmeci (2001) use quinquennial panel data on growth and investment shares for the post war period and show that the causality between fixed investment and growth runs in both directions, but the Granger causality from investment shares to growth rates is surprisingly negative. Hatemi-J and Irandoust (2002) study the causality between fixed investment and economic growth for several industrialized countries individually using the vector autoregression (VAR) model. Their results show that fixed investment and economic growth are causally related in the long run for each country: causality in Canada and Italy is bidirectional; direction of causality in Germany is from fixed investment to economic growth; in France, Sweden, and the UK, causality is running from growth to fixed investment. Ghali and Al-Mutawa's (1999) causality study on each of the G-7 countries also suggest that the causal relationship between investment and growth varies significantly across countries and may run in either direction.

The importance of capital accumulation in determining output growth has also been tested using growth-accounting procedure. The results from these studies in general show that differences in physical capital accounts for little of the international differences in output. King and Levin (1994) and Hall and Jones (1999) conducted growth accounting separately on more than 100 countries, and both studies showed that international differences in per capita capital explain little of the differences in per capita output across countries. However, King and Levine do find a strong and robust association between the ratio of investment to GDP and economic growth. In almost all the studies using growth accounting procedures, Solow residual, sometimes also termed as technological progress or total factor productivity (TFP), accounts for the bulk of cross-country growth differences. Some of the theoretical explanations of the Solow residual includes technology, externalities, and adoption of lower cost production methods (Easterly and Levine, 2001). Hall and Jones (1999) suggest that the differences in the Solow residual can be explained by differences in institutions and government policies, which they call "social infrastructure".

If Solow residual is viewed as the social infrastructure of a country, the level of physical capital stock is expected to be highly correlated with the Solow residual in a market economy. If this is the case, then the emphasis on physical capital stock is not misplaced. An economy with a well-developed social infrastructure is certainly an attractive destination for both domestic and foreign investments. At the same time, a high level of investment also serves to strengthen the social infrastructure of an economy. Social infrastructure and physical capital are also dependent on each other to carry out economic development. On its own, social infrastructure is not enough to generate growth; it would have to be combined with physical capital and other resources to produce economic development. Similarly, in the absence of adequate social infrastructure, an increase in capital stock would probably not result in an increase in GDP. This partly explains the ineffectiveness of foreign aid in spurring economic development of many developing countries. Thus, capital accumulation is still relevant, though not the only, ingredient of economic development. The other critical ingredient is social infrastructure. Both are likely to be closely correlated.

Singapore experienced very rapid increase in GDP between the 1960s and 1990s on the back of sharp increases in factor inputs. However, Krugman (1994) and Young (1995) dismiss the spectacular rise of Singapore's GDP by emphasizing that Singapore's TFP growth was negligible and that the high economic growth was only driven by resource accumulation. Krugman even predicts that Singapore could face a "Soviet-style" growth collapse. This chapter disagrees with Krugman and Young, and takes the view that a sharp increase in capital accumulation during the development process of a developing country is necessary to fuel current and future economic growth.

This chapter extends Lim's S-Curve hypothesis and postulates that capital accumulation of an economy also follows an S-Curve as the economy develops. Thus, an economy at Stage 1 of economic development would have a low level of per capita capital stock and a low rate of capital accumulation. Rate of capital accumulation would gain momentum as the economy enters Stage 2 of economic development. An economy at Stage 3 would enjoy a high level of per capita capital stock but its rate of capital accumulation, although still positive, would gradually decline. Implicitly assumed in the hypothesis of S-Curve of capital accumulation is that capital accumulation is strongly associated with output growth. The hypothesis suggests that a newly industrializing economy would experience rapid accumulation of capital, and this rate of capital growth would slowly taper off as the economy develops. This sharp increase in capital accumulation is necessary to fuel further economic growth. It is further postulated that the growth rate of capital stock is likely to outpace that of GDP during the early phase of industrialization. As a result of this S-Curve of capital accumulation, the incremental capital-output ratio (ICOR) and the average capital-output ratio (ACOR) of the economy are first likely to increase, and then gradually decrease as the economy ascends the development ladder. Some researchers regard an increasing level or a high level of ICOR as a sign of capital inefficiency; the S-Curve of capital accumulation shows that this is just part and parcel of economic development.

The outline of this chapter is as follows: Section 4.2 puts forth the hypothesis of the S-Curve of capital accumulation. Section 4.3 briefly reviews the concepts of ICOR and ACOR, and postulates the probable patterns of ICOR and ACOR as an economy develops. Section 4.4 uses cross-country data from 60 countries to ascertain the relationships between (i) capital level and output level, (ii) capital growth and output growth, and (iii) ACOR and output level. Section 4.5 presents a case study of Singapore. It shows that the development experience of Singapore concurs with the hypothesis of the S-Curve of capital accumulation. The long-term causal relationship between Singapore's capital stock and its GDP is also tested and found to be positive and bi-directional. Section 4.6 revisits the issue of TFP growth and capital growth, and reasons that in the case of Singapore, strong growth in physical capital is critical for the high economic growth achieved. Moreover, as Singapore's economy matures, contribution from physical capital diminishes, while contributions from TFP and human capital increase. The conclusion is given at the end of this chapter.

## 4.2. Hypothesis of the S-Curve of Capital Accumulation

In a framework similar to that of the S-Curve hypothesis, it is hypothesized that the accumulation of physical capital of an economy, as it develops, also takes the shape of an S-Curve. In Stage I of the development process, a turtle economy is likely to have a low level of per capita capital stock and a slow rate of capital growth. As the turtle economy transforms into a horse economy, the accumulation of capital gains momentum, and the level of per capita capital stock increases. As the horse economy graduates to become an elephant economy, the level of per capita capital stock would be high, but the rate of capital accumulation would slow down. The graphical representation of the S-Curve of capital accumulation and the S-Curve of output is shown in Fig. 4.1.

It is further hypothesized that during the early phase of industrialization of a horse economy, the growth rate of capital stock would outpace that of output. This is illustrated by the steeper slope of the S-Curve of the per capita capital stock during the earlier part of Stage II. The difference between these two growth rates is expected to narrow as the horse economy matures.

### 4.2.1. *Stage I: Low capital stock, low capital growth*

An underdeveloped turtle economy is likely to have a low level of per capita capital stock. This is intuitive as capital investment needs to be

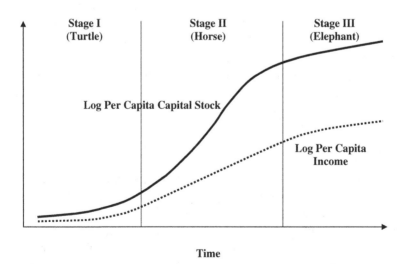

**Fig. 4.1.** S-Curve of capital accumulation.

financed out of savings from income, both of which are lacking in the poor countries. In addition, foreign investment is likely to be scarce in the absence of investment-conducive policies. Growth rate of per capita capital stock is also expected to be low since governments of developing countries often have limited tax-collecting and revenue-generating capabilities, and this lack of funds will restrict the governments' expenditure on infrastructural and developmental investment.

### 4.2.2. *Stage II: Middle capital stock, high capital growth*

On the other hand, for a turtle economy to metamorphose into a rapidly-industrializing horse economy, the domestic growth engine of the economy, as driven by its entrepreneurs, workers and government, would have undergone colossal transformation. An enterprising business community, a better-educated workforce, investment-conducive policies, and a lower cost structure as compared to the developed nation would serve as a magnet for both foreign and domestic direct investment. Two positive cycles of circular cumulative causation would also be set in motion. Firstly, the influx of foreign investment would provide increased business opportunities to domestic producers, thereby inducing further domestic investment in the economy. Secondly, as the fiscal position of the government improves, the government will be able to invest more heavily in the development of physical infrastructure and human capital. This could further enhance the attractiveness of the country as a destination of direct investment. As the economy gallops on the highway of economic development, capital investment by both the private and public sectors would increase rapidly.

### 4.2.3. *Stage III: High capital stock, low capital growth*

A highly-developed elephant economy that has experienced continued capital accumulation over prolonged periods will have a high level of per capita capital stock. Capital growth rate, however, is likely to slow down. The enormous stock of public sector's infrastructure that was built up over the long development process implies that the choices of investment in a developed country are increasingly limited. The social need for additional infrastructural investment would be small and the social returns on the new investment would be low. As a result, public sector's investment rate is likely to be low. At the same time, due to the high cost of production in the developed countries, direct investment, especially from the manufacturing sector, would flow from the expensive developed countries to the cheaper developing countries. This tendency is compounded by the fact that the developed economy is also saturated with private sector investment, such that diminishing returns set in. Investment capital would thus travel to countries that provide higher returns. In fact, many industrial towns in the developed countries face the constant threat of their industrial base hollowing out. All these explain the low rate of capital growth in the developed country.

## 4.3. Capital-Output Ratios and Economic Development

### 4.3.1. *Factors influencing level of ICOR*

The incremental capital-output ratio (ICOR) is defined as the amount of additional capital stock ($\Delta K$) needed to increase national output by one unit ($\Delta Y$), or $ICOR = \Delta K/\Delta Y$. Typically, ICOR is around 2–4 for developing countries (Gianaris, 1970), although it is not unusual to see economies with ICOR lower than 2 or higher than 6.

There are three important factors that influence the levels of ICOR. Firstly, if capital is assumed to be homogenous, ICOR is simply determined by the efficiency in the utilization of additional capital. Thus the lower the marginal productivity of capital, the higher the level of ICOR, and vice versa. Inefficiency in the utilization of capital could stem from many sources, such as inefficiency in the areas of organization, administration and production, and inappropriate adoption of capital-intensive production processes in labor-surplus developing countries.

Secondly, since capital is heterogeneous in the real world, the composition mix of capital stock would affect the level of ICOR of a country. For example, a country that is investing heavily in capital-intensive sectors such as transport networks, air and sea ports, and housing and electricity grids would have a much higher national-wide ICOR than a country whose investment is skewed towards fixed assets such as machinery and transport equipment. Similarly, a country with a large transportation and communication sector is likely to have a higher

ICOR than a country that has a large manufacturing sector. In this instance, the higher level of ICOR does not imply inefficiency in the utilization of additional capital. Moreover, different investment types have different service lives and different spin-off effects on the economy.

Thirdly, the stage of development of a country would also affect the level of ICOR and ACOR. A developing country is likely to have surplus labor and is thus likely to engage in labor-intensive production processes. This would give rise to low ICOR and ACOR. A developed country, on the other hand, is likely to have surplus capital and its production processes are likely to be capital-intensive. This would result in a higher ICOR and ACOR. During the long transition period, as a developing economy gradually transforms into a developed economy, there would be increasing substitution of capital for labor as a consequence of increasing labor cost. A high and rising ICOR during this period is thus part and parcel of the economic development process.

Although it is a combination of factors that influences the level of ICOR, a high level of ICOR has often been interpreted as a sign of inefficiency of investment, and an increasing ICOR as worsening efficiency in the utilization of additional capital. Such interpretations are commonly found in economic dictionaries, newspaper reports and even journal articles. For instance, Jun (2003) in his paper on investment and investment efficiency of China wrote, "A direct and simple measurement of investment efficiency at aggregate level may be carried out by calculating its so-called ICOR, which is the reciprocal of the marginal productivity of capital stock". Jun then compared the ICOR of China with those of the "little dragons" and "little tigers" of East Asia and noted that these countries, with the exception of Hong Kong, have experienced an upward sloping of ICOR between the 1970s and 1990s. He then concluded that "China's ICOR had trended downward since 1979, suggesting a better performance than most East Asian NIEs and emerging economies for the similar stage of development".

This "direct and simple" interpretation of ICOR, however, may be flawed. When comparing ICOR of two countries, a lower ICOR could be associated with greater efficiency in the use of incremental capital, provided both countries are at similar stages of development and have similar investment mix. In the absence of prior knowledge of investment composition, a straightforward comparison of ICOR could lead to misleading conclusions on capital efficiency. On the other hand, comparing sectoral ICOR of the same sector from different countries could be a more fruitful exercise, especially if the countries are at similar stage of development. In addition, inter-temporal comparison of ICOR and ACOR of a country could throw light on the structural transformation of the country.

### 4.3.2. *Relationship between ICOR and ACOR*

The average capital-output ratio (ACOR) is defined as the total capital stock $(K)$ required to produce the total output $(Y)$, or $ACOR = K/Y$. It is a measurement of the average productivity of the entire capital stock, assuming that the capital stock is fully utilized. Underutilization of capital stock, say during a recession, would lead to an overstated ACOR.

If a linear relationship is assumed between capital and output such that $K = \alpha Y$, an assumption used in the Harrod–Domar growth model, then it would imply that ICOR equals to ACOR and both ICOR and ACOR are the same constant.

However, it is evident from empirical studies that ICOR is often not equal to ACOR, and they are not constant. As shown in Fig. 4.2, a rising

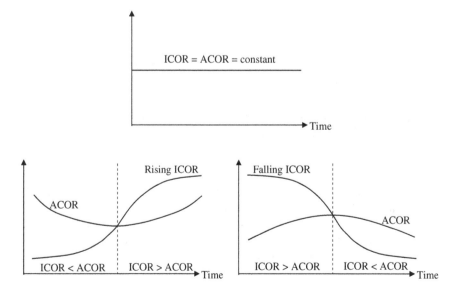

**Fig. 4.2.** Relationship between ICOR and ACOR.

ICOR could be accompanied by an increasing or decreasing ACOR. If the ICOR is higher than the ACOR in absolute value, the ACOR will be increasing; if the ICOR is lower than the ACOR in absolute value, the ACOR will be decreasing even if the ICOR is increasing.

Similarly, a declining ICOR could go hand-in-hand with a growing ACOR or a falling ACOR. If the ICOR is larger than the ACOR in absolute value, the ACOR will be increasing regardless of a falling ICOR; if the ICOR is smaller than the ACOR in absolute value, ACOR will be decreasing.

ICOR and ACOR are also related to each other through the growth rate of capital and the growth rate of output as shown below:

$$\frac{\Delta K}{\Delta Y} = \frac{\frac{\Delta K}{K} \times K}{\frac{\Delta Y}{Y} \times Y}$$

$$\Rightarrow \text{ICOR} = \frac{\frac{\Delta K}{K}}{\frac{\Delta Y}{Y}} \times \text{ACOR}$$

Thus, ICOR will be higher than ACOR if the growth rate of capital is higher than that of output. This in turn will lead to an increasing ACOR; and vice-versa.

### 4.3.3. *S-Curve of capital accumulation and its implied ICOR and ACOR*[1]

A turtle economy is likely to have low levels of ICOR and ACOR as production processes are likely to be labor-intensive. This is due to the

---

[1] This section assumes that economies are generally efficient in utilizing their capital, which is likely to be true for the more developed market economies than otherwise. In this case, the levels of ICOR and ACOR of the economies are expected to be influenced by their stages of development and the composition mixes of their capital stock. If inefficiencies in the utilization of capital are prevalence in the turtle economies, the ICOR and ACOR would then be much higher than those described in this section.

general lack of supply of capital and the excess supply of labor in a turtle economy.

A horse economy is likely to experience increasing ICOR for three reasons. Firstly, a horse economy is expected to undergo a period of rapid increase in capital investment as private sector's investment pours into the economy. ICOR is given by the ratio of investment rate to GDP growth rate, or ICOR $= (I/Y)/(\Delta Y/Y)$. In the short to medium term, as the investment rate expands rapidly while the output growth lags behind, ICOR will be pushed up inevitably. This is because output to be generated from this influx of investment is expected to be reaped over a longer term. Secondly, as the excess labor in the economy is exhausted, production process has to become increasingly capital-intensive. This again will lead to an increasing ICOR. Thirdly, the government would be undertaking large-scale infrastructural projects which have higher levels of ICOR. However, physical infrastructure has a much longer longevity than other forms of fixed-asset investment such as machinery and equipment, which would mean that the benefits (in terms of output generation) of the infrastructural projects would extend over a much longer period. If ICOR is higher than ACOR, which will be the case when capital growth outpaces GDP growth, then the horse economy would have both increasing ICOR and increasing ACOR. As the horse economy gradually matures into an elephant economy, the rate of increase of ICOR will slow down, and the level of ICOR may even start to decline.

An elephant economy with its high level of accumulated investment is likely to have a low investment rate. At the same time, the elephant economy continues to reap the returns of earlier investment, especially those in infrastructure and buildings that have very long service lives. Thus, the ICOR of an elephant economy is likely to be falling, albeit gradually, as the investment rate falls faster than the GDP growth rate. However, as the production processes adopted in an elephant economy contains much higher capital intensity, the ICOR of the elephant economy would be higher than that of a turtle economy. ACOR is likely to be inching up very gradually for the elephant economy, and may eventually stabilize or even decline.

A probable pattern of the ACOR and the ICOR changing over the development process of a country is given in Fig. 4.3.

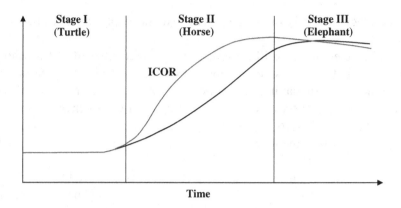

**Fig. 4.3.**   S-Curve and capital-output ratios.

## 4.4. International Evidence on Capital Accumulation and Economic Development

If the hypothesis of S-Curve of capital accumulation is correct, empirical studies on capital and economic development should present the following evidence:

1. Output level is positively associated with the level of physical capital; the higher the level of physical capital, the higher is the level of output.
2. Output growth is positively associated with the growth of physical capital. Capital growth is most rapid for a horse economy; growth rate slows down as the horse economy turns into an elephant economy.
3. A turtle economy is likely to have low levels of ICOR and ACOR. A horse economy is likely to have an increasing ICOR and ACOR. The levels of ICOR and ACOR of an elephant economy are likely to stabilize and could eventually gradually decline.
4. As both the private and public sectors of a horse economy undertake substantial investment, the GDP growth of a horse economy would lag behind the growth of its capital stock. On the other hand, the GDP growth rate of an elephant economy would be higher than its capital stock growth rate, as the elephant economy continues to reap the benefits of earlier investments.

Cross-country data will be used in this sector to provide evidence to the first three points.

### 4.4.1. *Data source*

There are several databases that provide internationally comparable data on capital stock, such as the King and Levine Data Set, the Nehru Dhareshwar Data Set and the Penn-World Table (PWT) 5.6. King and Levine (1994) and Nehru and Dhareshwar (1993) provide capital stock estimates for about 100 countries from 1950 to the late 1980s. Both sets of data were created using the Perpetual Inventory Method (PIM) — initial capital stocks of countries in 1950 were first estimated, aggregate investment data from the subsequent years were then accumulated while assuming a certain depreciation rate. Both the King and Levine Data Set and the Nehru Dhareshwar Data Set are available from the World Bank's web site. The third data set, PWT 5.6,[2] provides data on "non-residential capital stock per worker" for 63 countries from 1965 to 1992 using the PIM. Although the number of countries covered by the PWT 5.6 is smaller, it has one advantage over the other two data sets: instead of using aggregate investment, PWT 5.6 utilized capital stock components, namely machinery and equipment, non-residential and other construction, in its computation of capital stock. Residential construction is not included. The capital stock data from PWT 5.6 is used in the following analysis.

### 4.4.2. *Capital level and output level*

Using GDP per capita as a proxy for economic development, it is evident from Fig. 4.4 that per capita income level increases as capital stock per worker grows. This is as expected, and is in line with the hypothesis of S-Curve of capital accumulation. The two variables are highly correlated, with a correlation coefficient of 0.90.

GDP per capita (GDPPC) is then regressed against capital stock per worker (KPW). The regression result and the corresponding *t*-statistics

---

[2] The latest version of the Penn-World Table, PWT 6.1, was released in 2002. However, data on capital stock are not available yet.

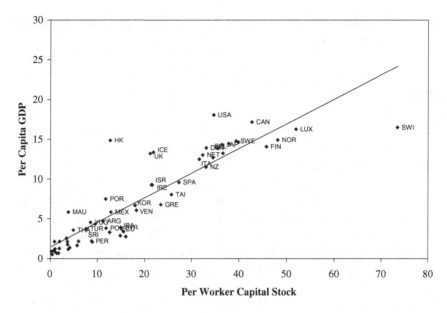

**Fig. 4.4.**   Cross-country comparison of capital stock and GDP ('000 International $ in 1985 prices), 1990.

*Source*: Computed using data from PWT 5.6.

(in parentheses) are as follows: Both coefficients are highly significant at 5% significance level and the coefficient of determination is 81%:

$$GDPPC = 1.44 + 0.310\ KPW$$
$$(2.95)\ (15.58)$$

$$R^2 = 0.81$$

The result suggests that an increase in per worker capital stock of one International dollar led to, on average, an increase of about 31 International cents of real per capita GDP.


### 4.4.3. *Capital growth and output growth*

21 countries are categorized according to the three growth phases of the S-Curve hypothesis. Eight developed nations, four newly industrializing

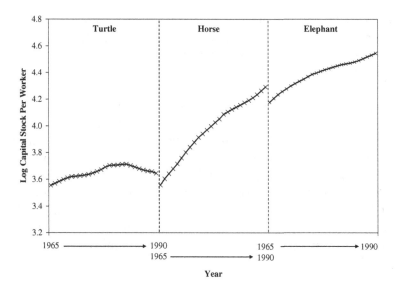

**Fig. 4.5.** Time paths of average log capital stock per worker of turtle, horse and elephant economies, 1965–1990.

*Source*: Computed using data from PWT 5.6.

economies and Japan,[3] and eight developing countries are selected to represent the elephant economies, the horse economies, and the turtle economies respectively. The elephant economies selected are: Canada, Denmark, France, Germany, New Zealand, Sweden, United Kingdom and USA. Hong Kong, Japan, South Korea, Taiwan and Thailand are chosen to represent the horse economies. The turtle economies are: Kenya, Madagascar, Malawi, Peru, the Philippines, Sierra Leone, Venezuela and Zambia. The time paths of the averages of log of capital stock per worker of these three groups of countries are plotted in Fig. 4.5.

It is evident from Fig. 4.5 the fastest growing horse economies were also the countries that experienced the most rapid growth in capital stock over the last 35 years. Capital growth in the horse economies is significantly faster than those of the turtle economies (which exhibited no

---

[3] Although Japan is very much an elephant economy now, it can be considered as a horse economy between 1965 and the late 1980s.

obvious trend) and the elephant economies (which increased gradually). Furthermore, it is also evident from the time series that capital stock per worker increases as an economy develops, the same evidence that was borne out in Section 4.4.2 using cross-sectional data.

The three panels of time series when placed side-by-side gives an indication of the time trend of per worker capital stock as an economy progresses from a turtle economy to a horse economy and finally to an elephant economy. In other words, capital growth is low and erratic and may even turn negative for the turtle economy. As the economy is transformed into a horse economy, capital growth is robust and rapid, resulting in rapid growth in output level. The causality between output growth and capital growth can be bi-directional of course. As the economy gradually matures into an elephant one, capital stock, although still growing, will grow at a slower pace. This, in essence, sketches the S-Curve of capital accumulation.

### 4.4.4. *ACOR and economic development*

Empirical evidence has generally shown that ACOR is positively related to per capita income and that ACOR tends to increase as countries develop. In an exercise to explore the association of ACOR with the level of development, King and Levine (1994) regress the ACOR during the 1980s on the ratio of income per capita relative to income per capita in the United States for the cross-section of 105 non-oil countries. Their regression result suggests that richer countries have higher capital-output ratios.

ACOR can be computed by dividing the capital stock of a country by its GDP. "Capital Stock per Worker" and "GDP per Worker" from the PWT 5.6 is used to compute figures on ACOR. Using GDP per capita as a proxy of economic development, ACOR for 60 countries in 1990 is plotted against their respective per capita GDP (see Fig. 4.6). The correlation coefficient between the two variables is moderate at 0.430. However, there is some broad trend that indicates higher level of ACOR for countries with higher level of per capita GDP. Almost all the high-income countries have high levels of ACOR, with the exception of Hong Kong, which was a colony until 1997. Many of the medium-income economies, such as Taiwan, Greece, South Korea, Spain and Ireland, have high levels of ACOR that are comparable to those of the high-income countries.

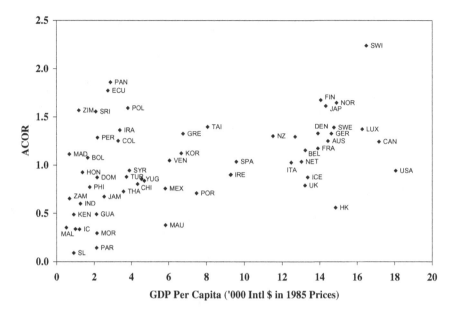

**Fig. 4.6.** Cross-country comparison of ACOR, 1990.

*Source*: Computed using data from PWT 5.6.

The levels of ACOR of the low-income countries span almost evenly over a very wide range; Panama has an ACOR of 1.9, which is higher than most of the high-income countries. As mentioned earlier, inefficiency in the utilization of capital is one of the factors that could result in a high level of ACOR, a situation that is expected to be more prevalent in the lesser-developed countries. However, we can also see from Fig. 4.6 that there is a significant portion of low-income countries with very low levels of ACOR.

Figure 4.7 plots the time paths of the averages of ACOR of the three categories of countries from 1965 to 1990. The eight elephant economies and the eight turtle economies used in Fig. 4.5 are also used here. Hong Kong is removed from the sample of horse economies as its very low level of ACOR could be considered as an outlier. All the three categories of economies experienced an increase in ACOR over the last 25 years, indicating a general increase in capital intensity of the global economy. Out of the three categories of economies, the increase in ACOR experienced by the horse economy is the largest. Furthermore, the level of ACOR of

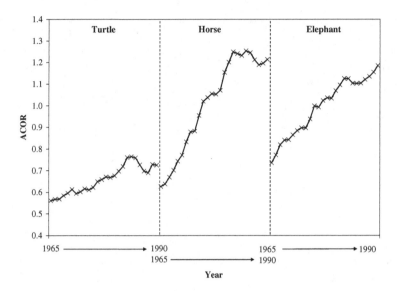

**Fig. 4.7.**   Time paths of average ACOR of turtle, horse and elephant economies, 1965–1990.

*Source*: Computed using data from PWT 5.6.

the horse economy overtook that of the elephant economy in the early 1970s and remained higher than the ACOR of the elephant economy ever since.

## 4.5.  Capital Accumulation and Economic Development of Singapore

### 4.5.1.  *Singapore's S-Curve of capital accumulation*

Data on Singapore's capital stock are constructed from data on Gross Fixed Capital Formation (GFCF) at 2000 prices using the Perpetual Inventory Method (PIM). Straight-line depreciation is assumed and the assumptions on the longevity of various categories of capital stock follow those used by Singapore's Department of Statistics (DOS) in their computation of the capital stock of Singapore (Department of Statistics, 1997; OECD, 2001). Details on the construction of the data series of the capital stock of Singapore can be found in Appendix 1.

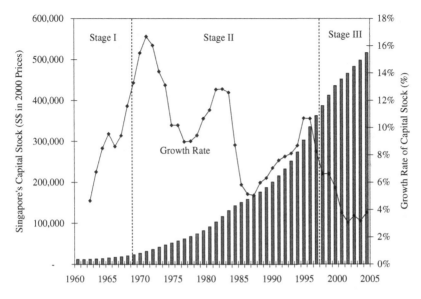

**Fig. 4.8.** Singapore's capital stock (S$ in 2000 prices), 1960–2006.

*Source*: Writer's estimate using raw data from CEIC database.

Figure 4.8 presents the estimated capital stock of Singapore from 1960 to 2006. The general trend in the figure conforms to the hypothesis of the S-Curve of capital accumulation. It is evident from Fig. 4.8 that the accumulation of capital got to a slow start during the early phase of Singapore's economic development (low level and low growth of capital). The build up of capital gained momentum in the late 1960s, signaling Singapore's entrance into a new phase of rapid industrialization (medium level and high growth of capital). The growth of capital stock appears to have slowed down since 1998 (high level and low growth of capital).

Figure 4.9 sub-divides the capital stock in Singapore by institutional sectors — public and private. It can be seen from Fig. 4.9 that the intensive pace of capital accumulation by the public sector in the 1970s and early 1980s fizzled out around mid-1980s. Between 1970 and 1986, public sector's capital stock grew by an average of 11.6% per annum; the average annual growth rate of capital stock was drastically reduced to 4.9% since 1987. This is consistent with our earlier view that public sector's investment tends to decline as an economy develops. On the other hand, average

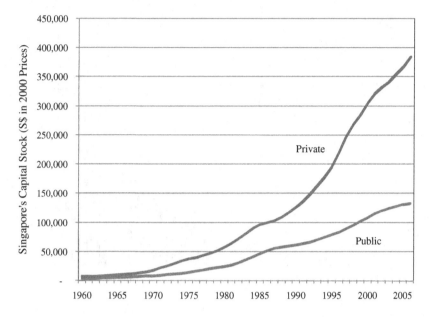

**Fig. 4.9.**   Singapore public sector's and private sector's capital stock (S$ in 2000 prices), 1960–2006.

*Source*: Writer's estimate using raw data from CEIC database.

annual growth rate of private sector's capital stock fell by a smaller degree; capital stock growth rate decreased from 11.7% per annum between 1970 and 1986 to 7.0% per annum between 1987 and 2006.

### 4.5.2. *Singapore's capital and economic development*

As discussed in the earlier sections, the S-Curve of capital accumulation hypothesized that output level is positively associated with the level of physical capital stock and output growth is positively associated with growth of physical capital stock. Furthermore, the GDP growth of a horse economy would lag behind the growth of its capital stock, while the GDP growth of an elephant economy would be higher than its capital stock growth. These propositions are in line with the development experience of Singapore.

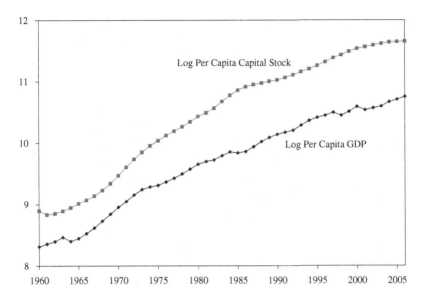

**Fig. 4.10.**   Singapore's log per capita GDP and log per capita capital stock (S$ in 2000 prices), 1960–2006.

*Source*: Writer's estimate using raw data from CEIC database.

Singapore's per capita GDP has grown in tandem with the increase in the per capita capital stock over the years (see Fig. 4.10). In 1960, when Singapore was still a turtle economy, per capita GDP and per capita capital stock were both very low at only S$4,080 and S$7,290 respectively, measured in 2000 prices. Singapore began its metamorphosis into a horse economy from the mid-1960s. And since the mid-1960s to late-1990s, Singapore's per capita capital stock grew rapidly, as did its per capita GDP. However, it can be seen from Fig. 4.10 that the growth of both the per capita GDP and the per capita capital stock appears to be tapering off in the late 1990s. It may indicate that Singapore is gradually becoming an elephant economy.

Singapore's per capita GDP and per capita capital stock are highly correlated, with the Spearman's correlation coefficient at 0.99. However, there may be spurious correlation between these two variables as both are also highly correlated with time. Thus, the correlation test between the first difference of per capita GDP and the first difference of capital stock are run, and they are also found to be highly correlated. The Spearman's correlation coefficient is obtained as 0.62. This is equivalent to saying that the changes of GDP and the changes of capital stock are highly correlated.

It can also be seen from Fig. 4.10 that the vertical distance between the two curves is widening over time; this indicates a rising ACOR. This is in agreement with our earlier proposition that the per capita capital stock of a horse economy would rise faster than its per capita GDP.

Table 4.1 reaffirms the observation made in Fig. 4.10. Since 1970, the growth rates of per capita capital stock were consistently higher than that of the GDP. Furthermore, the difference between the two sets of growth rates narrowed as time went by. This lends support to the earlier proposition that the increase in GDP will catch up with that of the capital stock during the later phase of the rapid development stage of an economy, as the economy continues to reap the benefits of earlier investments.

### 4.5.3. *Granger causality between Singapore's capital accumulation and GDP growth*

Although it has been shown in the preceding sub-section that the change in Singapore's per capita capital is highly correlated with the change in Singapore's per capital output, correlation is not the same as causality. It would be interesting to find out the direction of causality between Singapore's capital stock and its GDP level. Granger Causality Bivariate

**Table 4.1.**   Average annual growth rates of Singapore's per capita GDP and per capita capital stock (in 2000 prices).

|  | Per capita GDP (%) | Per capita capital stock (%) |
|---|---|---|
| 1960–1969 | 6.0 | 5.1 |
| 1970–1979 | 7.1 | 10.2 |
| 1980–1989 | 4.9 | 6.5 |
| 1990–1999 | 4.3 | 5.3 |
| 2000–2006 | 2.7 | 1.9 |
| 1960–2006 | 5.4 | 6.2 |

*Source*: Writer's estimate using raw data from CEIC database.

VECM Test is used in this sub-section to establish the causality between Singapore's capital stock ($K$) and GDP ($Y$).

While the Augmented Dickey–Fuller (ADF) test shows that unit root exists in both the data series of $K_t$ and $Y_t$, the first differences of $K_t$ and $Y_t$ are found to be stationary. The Johansen co-integration test shows that both $K_t$ and $Y_t$ are co-integrated; that is, there exists a long-term equilibrium relationship between capital stock and GDP.

A Bivariate Vector Error Correction Model (VECM) is set up to establish the causality between capital stock and GDP:

$$\Delta Y_t = \mu + \theta(Y_{t-1} - \alpha - \beta K_{t-1}) + \sum \alpha_i \Delta K_{t-i} + \sum \beta_j \Delta Y_{t-j} + U_{yt}$$

$$\Delta K_t = \omega + \phi(Y_{t-1} - \alpha - \beta K_{t-1}) + \sum \gamma_i \Delta K_{t-i} + \sum \delta_j \Delta Y_{t-j} + U_{mt}$$

A lag of 1 period is found to minimize the value of the Akaike's Information Criteria (AIC). The VECM estimates are given as follows:

| | |
|---|---|
| $\theta$ | −0.158* |
| $\phi$ | 0.055** |
| $\sum \alpha_i$ | −0.025 |
| $\sum \delta_i$ | 0.341* |

\* denotes significance at 1% level;
\** at 5% level.

The results of the VECM estimates show that there existed a positive and significant bi-directional long-term causal relationship between Singapore's capital stock and its GDP. In the short term, the granger causality ran from GDP growth to increase in capital stock. The granger causality from changes in capital stock to GDP growth is statistically insignificant.

### 4.5.4. *Singapore's capital-output ratios*

It was hypothesized in Section 4.3 that a turtle economy is likely to have low levels of ICOR and ACOR, a horse economy is likely to have increasing levels of ICOR and ACOR, and the levels of ICOR and ACOR of an elephant economy are likely to be lower than the horse economy but will still be significantly higher than those of the turtle economy.

Figure 4.11 shows the variability of Singapore's ACOR from 1960 to 2006. Level of ACOR was steadily rising from less than 1.8 in the early 1960s to about 2.8 in the early 2000s. There were four prominent upsurges of the ACOR over the last 47 years, and they coincided with the recessionary years of Singapore: 1964, 1985, 1998 and 2001. During recession, output falls sharply while capital stock remains relatively stable, resulting in an underutilization of capital. This leads to a sudden increase in ACOR, which is not representative.

It can be seen from Fig. 4.11 that Singapore's ACOR expanded rapidly in the first 20 years after Singapore attained independence in 1965. This is in line with the hypothesis of the S-Curve of capital accumulation — a horse economy would experience increasing ACOR (and ICOR) during the early stages of industrialization. The steady increase of the ACOR ran out of steam in the late 1980s, and the ACOR was range-bound between 2.3 and 2.8 since 1988. The level of ACOR in 2006 was 2.5. Given Singapore's advanced stage of development, the future level of ACOR is expected to hover around 2.6 and may even gradually decline.

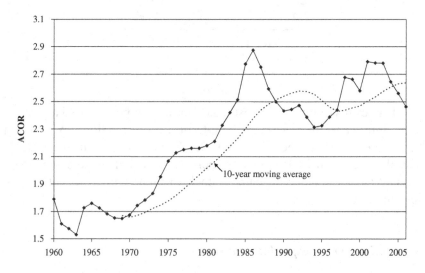

**Fig. 4.11.**    Singapore's average capital-output ratio, 1960–2006.

*Source*: Writer's estimate using raw data from CEIC database.

## 4.6. Capital Growth and Total Factor Productivity Growth of Singapore

Under the framework of growth accounting, economic growth is attributable to increases in factor inputs and improvements in total factor productivity (TFP). Factor inputs commonly included in growth accounting exercises are physical capital, labor force and human capital,[4] while TFP is measured as the residual of the growth equation after accounting for the increases in factor inputs. TFP would include both technological progress and enhanced efficiency, although the contributions from these two factors are not distinguishable from the derived estimates.

In almost all studies on growth accounting, such as Hall and Jones (1999) and King and Levine (1994), TFP is found to account for the bulk of cross-country growth differences, while differences in physical capital account for little of the international differences in output growth. Thus, the long-term growth potential of an economy is often determined by its ability to achieve and sustain a high level of TFP growth.

Studies on decomposition of Singapore's economic growth, such as Tsao (1982), Young (1992, 1995), Rao and Lee (1995), Koh, Rahman and Tan (2002) and Hsieh (2002), have all pointed to the overwhelming importance of capital accumulation in propelling the growth of Singapore, and the smaller degree of contribution made by TFP growth. In addition, some of the earlier studies, such as those by Tsao (1982) and Young (1992, 1995), concluded that Singapore's TFP growth rates were negligible. The high level of capital growth and the corresponding extremely low level of TFP growth have prompted Krugman (1994) and Young (1995) to cast doubt on the sustainability of Singapore's economic growth; Krugman even predicted that Singapore could face a "Soviet-style" growth collapse.

There are two questions concerning the issue of TPF growth and capital growth. Firstly, was Singapore's TFP growth rates as low as those computed by Tsao (1982) and Young (1992, 1995)? Secondly, is high capital growth the boon or bane of sustainable economic growth?

The first question is a technical one that requires a technical answer. Young (1995) estimated that out of the 8.7% average GDP growth rate from 1966 to 1990, the growth in TFP averaged only 0.2%. The extremely low level of TFP growth of Singapore obtained by Young stems from his

---

[4] Human capital is usually measured as a function of number of years of schooling.

assumptions about the factor shares in the production function. Young estimates the output elasticity of capital of Singapore to be around 0.5, substantially higher than the 0.35 in a typical economy (Eggertsson, 2004). Eggertsson cites the estimates of factor shares computed by Bosworth and Collins (2003) and Sarel (1997), and reasons that $\alpha = 0.35$ is a more appropriate figure. Using the assumption of $\alpha = 0.35$, Eggertsson (2004) shows that Singapore's average TFP growth over the period 1960–2003 was at 1.4%. Eggertsson's decomposition of the economic growth of Singapore is reproduced in Table 4.2. In addition, Eggertsson also shows that Singapore's TFP growth rates are comparable to, if not higher than, those of the other advanced and emerging economies (see Table 4.3). Other studies on decomposition of growth of Singapore by Wu and Thia (2002) and Hsieh (2002) have also reported a higher level of TFP growth than that reported by Young (1992). The reported TFP growth by Wu and Thia for 1990–2000 is 1.6%. Hsieh estimates TFP growth for the East Asian economies using the dual approach and finds that Singapore's TFP growth to be around 1.6% to 1.9% between 1968 and 1990.

On the question of whether high capital growth is the boon or bane of sustainable economic growth, the answer is less quantifiable but it is more intuitive. It can be seen from Table 4.2 that Singapore's growth since 1960 has been largely driven by capital accumulation; contribution from physical capital accounted for more than 50% of Singapore's output growth from 1960 to 2003. It is indisputable that the high rate of capital growth has contributed positively to the high economic growth rates and the rapid improvement in the living standards in Singapore. As pointed out by Ghesquiere (2006), "... notwithstanding the neoclassical concern about

**Table 4.2.** Sources of growth in Singapore, 1960–2003.

|                  | 1960–70     | 1970–80     | 1980–90    | 1990–03    | 1960–03    |
|------------------|-------------|-------------|------------|------------|------------|
| Output           | 9.4         | 8.6         | 7.2        | 6.2        | 7.7        |
| Physical capital | 5.6 (60%)   | 4.8 (56%)   | 3.2 (44%)  | 2.6 (42%)  | 4.0 (52%)  |
| Labor            | 1.9 (20%)   | 2.8 (33%)   | 2.2 (31%)  | 1.2 (19%)  | 2.0 (26%)  |
| Education        | 0.5 (5%)    | 0.1 (1%)    | 0.3 (4%)   | 0.8 (13%)  | 0.5 (6%)   |
| TFP              | 1.4 (15%)   | 0.9 (10%)   | 1.6 (22%)  | 1.6 (26%)  | 1.4 (18%)  |

*Note*: Figures in parenthesis refer to percentage contribution to output.
*Source*: Eggertsson (2004) and writer's own computation.

**Table 4.3.** International comparison of sources of growth, 1960–2000.

| | Singapore | East Asia less China[5] | United States | Industrial countries[6] |
|---|---|---|---|---|
| Output | 7.7 | 6.7 | 3.4 | 3.5 |
| Physical capital | 4.0 (52%) | 3.3 (49%) | 1.0 (29%) | 1.4 (40%) |
| Labor | 2.0 (26%) | 1.8 (27%) | 1.1 (32%) | 0.8 (23%) |
| Education | 0.5 (6%) | 0.5 (7%) | 0.3 (9%) | 0.3 (9%) |
| TFP | 1.4 (18%) | 1.0 (15%) | 0.9 (26%) | 1.0 (29%) |

*Notes* 1: Data on Singapore is for the period 1960–2003.
    2: Figures in parenthesis refer to percentage contribution to output.
*Source*: Eggertsson (2004) and writer's own computation.

diminishing returns…, high fixed capital formation can ensure high growth and rising living standards from low initial levels. The transition to the "steady state" when these forces become impotent can take several decades".

Furthermore, the high rate of capital accumulation has built for Singapore a strong physical foundation that serves as a platform for future growth. In other words, instead of being a hindrance, the strong growth in capital stock is likely to provide the impetus for future gain of TFP. It can be seen from Table 4.2 that the early strong contributions of physical capital and labor input have eased over time falling from 60% in the 1960s to 42% during 1990–2003, while TPF growth and contribution of human capital have gradually increased. During 1990–2003, TFP and human capital jointly accounted for almost 40% of Singapore's GDP, a level comparable to the contribution of physical capital.

If we were to deduce any lesson from Table 4.2, it would be that strong growth in physical capital is usually necessary for high economic growth of an economy during the early phase of its industrialization process. As the economy matures, the contribution from physical capital

---

[5] The seven East Asian countries are: Indonesia, Korea, Malaysia, the Philippines, Singapore, Taiwan, and Thailand.
[6] The 22 industrial countries are: Australia, Austria, Belgium, Canada, Denmark, Finland, France, Germany, Greece, Iceland, Ireland, Italy, Japan, Netherlands, New Zealand, Norway, Portugal, Spain, Sweden, Switzerland, United Kingdom, and the United States.

will diminish, and the contributions from TFP and human capital are likely to increase.

## 4.7. Conclusion

This chapter extends Lim's S-Curve hypothesis and postulates that capital accumulation of an economy also follows that of an S-Curve as the economy develops. An economy at its initial stage of economic development would have a low level and a low growth of capital stock; a rapidly industrializing economy would have a middle level and a high growth of capital stock; a matured industrialized economy would have a high level but a low growth of capital stock. As a result of this S-Curve of capital accumulation, the incremental capital-output ratio (ICOR) and the average capital-output ratio (ACOR) of the economy are likely to first increase, and then gradually decrease as the economy ascends the development ladder.

Using cross-country data from 60 countries, it is shown that:

1. Capital stock is highly correlated with output level;
2. Turtle economies (economies with low output level and low output growth) and elephant economies (economies with high output level but low output growth) experienced slower rate of capital accumulation, while horse economies (economies with middle level of output and high output growth) experienced faster rate of capital accumulation;
3. There is some broad trend that indicates that countries with higher level of per capita GDP have higher level of ACOR;
4. All three categories of economies: turtle, horse and elephant, experienced an increase in ACOR over the period 1965–1990, indicating a general increase in capital-intensity of the global economy. Out of the three categories of economies, the increase in ACOR experienced by the horse economy is the largest.

In addition, the case study of Singapore shows that the development experience of Singapore concurs with the hypothesis of the S-Curve of capital accumulation. Moreover, the long-term causal relationship between Singapore's capital stock and its GDP is found to be positive and bi-directional.

If the S-Curve hypothesis is correct, the following conclusions can be drawn:

1. An economy that is undergoing transformation from a turtle economy to a horse economy would experience rapid capital growth. As a result, the horse economy would have increasing ICOR and ACOR. This is part and parcel of the development process and does not necessarily mean that the horse economy is inefficient in utilizing its capital. ICOR would start to fall as the horse economy becomes an elephant economy. ACOR for the elephant economy may eventually stabilize or even decline.
2. Capital growth would slow down for a horse economy turning into an elephant economy, and would continue to slow down as the elephant economy matures. Thus, capital growth of a highly developed country would be lower than that of a newly industrializing country, and so would be the rate of GDP growth.
3. Capital accumulation remains a critical driver of growth of a developing economy. In addition, a high level of accumulated capital is likely to serve as the foundation for future gains in TFP. As the economy matures, the contribution from physical capital will diminish, while the contributions from TFP and human capital are likely to increase.

## 4.8. Appendix 1. Constructing Singapore's Capital Stock Data

Data on Gross Fixed Capital Formation (GFCF) at 1995 prices are available from 1960 onwards from the CEIC database. The GFCF data are classified by institutional sectors: public and private, and are divided into five categories: residential buildings, non-residential buildings, other construction and works, transport equipment, and machinery and equipment.

The widely-used Perpetual Inventory Method (PIM) is used to generate an estimate of Singapore's gross capital stock (GCS). The PIM accumulates past purchases of each asset type, and removes from the capital stock fixed assets that are scrapped upon reaching the end of their respective service lives. A depreciation function is applied to the GCS to calculate the depreciation, or the consumption, of fixed capital. The net capital stock (NCS) can then be obtained by subtracting accumulated capital consumption from the GCS.

**Table 4.4.**   Assumptions of Average Service Life.

| Asset class | Average service life (Year) |
| --- | :---: |
| Residential buildings | 80 |
| Non-residential buildings | 40 |
| Other construction and works | 40 |
| Transport equipment[8] | 15 |
| Machinery and equipment | 15 |

*Source*: OECD (2001).

Assumptions used in this paper are as follows[7]:

1. straight-line depreciation;
2. average service lives of assets ranging from 15 to 80 years (see Table 4.4);
3. average service lives do not vary over time, and are identical for all kinds of economic activities; and
4. simultaneous retirement of assets at the end of their respective service lives.

In order to obtain the initial benchmark estimate of Singapore's capital stock as at 1960, the methodology employed by Rao and Lee (1995) is used. It can be seen from Fig. 4.12 that except 1964 and 1965, which was a year of recession and a year after recession respectively, Singapore's ICOR between 1961 and 1970 was reasonably stable. The stability of ICOR could mean that the average ICOR approximates the average capital-output ratio (ACOR). From 1961 to 1963, the ICOR recorded was 1.7. 2.1 and 1.7, and the average over the three-year period was 1.86.

---

[7] The assumptions used in this paper are the same of those used by the Singapore's Department of Statistics (DOS) in their computation of the capital stock of Singapore (Department of Statistics, 1997; OECD, 2001). Capital stock data computed by the DOS is not available in the public domain.

[8] The DOS (1997) further classified transport equipment into three sub-categories: ships and boats, aircraft, and road vehicles. The assumed average service lives used by the DOS are 20 years, 15 years and 10 years respectively. As only aggregated figures on the Gross Fixed Capital Formation of transport equipment is available in the public domain, the average service life for transport equipment as an aggregate is assumed in this paper to be 15 years.

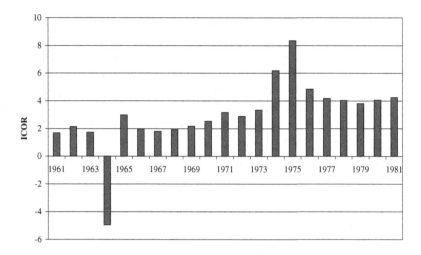

**Fig. 4.12.** Singapore's ICOR, 1961–1981.

*Source*: Computed using raw data from CEIC.

**Table 4.5.** Estimated Gross Capital Stock of Singapore in 1960 (S$ million in 1995 prices).

|  | Public | Private | Total |
|---|---|---|---|
| Residential buildings | 1,654 (13.1) | 4,013 (31.9) | 5,667 (45.1) |
| Non-residential buildings | 646 (5.1) | 1,052 (8.4) | 1,698 (13.5) |
| Other construction and works | 1,681 (13.4) | — | 1,681 (13.4) |
| Transport equipment | 71 (0.6) | 927 (7.4) | 998 (7.9) |
| Machinery and equipment | 335 (2.7) | 2,197 (17.5) | 2,532 (20.1) |
| Total | 4,387 (34.9) | 8,189 (65.1) | 12,576 |

*Source*: Writer's estimate using raw data from the CEIC database.

Thus, 1.86 is taken as an approximation of ACOR of Singapore's economy in 1960.

The ACOR of 1.86 for 1960 is then multiplied by the level of real GDP in 1960 (measured in 1995 prices). The estimated capital stock derived is S$12,600 million. In order to obtain a breakdown of capital stock by asset type, the investment share for 1960 was used. The capital stock estimates for 1960 are shown in Table 4.5. The figures in the parentheses are the percentage shares of total capital stock.

However, as the information on the timing of purchases of assets included in the initial benchmark estimates of capital stock is not available, straight-line depreciation cannot be used for 1960's capital stock estimates. The only depreciation method that can be used when information on the timing of investment is not available is geometric depreciation. Thus, geometric depreciation is assumed for the initial benchmark estimates of capital stock. The Hulten–Wykoff's (1981) depreciation estimates as aggregated by Young (1992) are adopted. The depreciation rates are: 1.3% for residential buildings, 2.9% for non-residential buildings and other construction and works, 18.2% for transport equipment, and 13.8% for machinery and equipment.

Gross capital stock (GCS) for each asset category from 1960 onwards is computed using the following formula:

$$K_t^G = K_{t-1}^G + I_t^G - R_t,$$

where $K_t^G$ is the gross capital stock at the end of year $t$, $K_{t-1}^G$ is the gross capital stock at the end of year $t-1$, $I_t^G$ is the gross investment or gross fixed capital formation during the year $t$, and   is the retirement during year $t$.

As a linear depreciation function with simultaneous exit is assumed, $D_t$ the depreciation of an asset category in year $t$ is given by:

$$D_t = \frac{\left(K_{t-1}^G + I_t^G - R_t\right)}{T} = \frac{K_t^G}{T}.$$

The difference between the net capital stock (NCS) and the GCS is the accumulated depreciation. NCS for each asset category at the end of year $t$ $(K_t^N)$ is computed using the following formula:

$$K_t^N = K_{t-1}^N + I_t^G - D_t.$$

Table 4.6 gives the gross capital stock and net capital stock estimates of Singapore from 1960 to 2006.

Capital stock data used in this paper refers to the net capital stock (NCS). Gross capital stock (GCS) is the capital stock of a country before depreciation is taken into account, while NCS is the capital stock net of

**Table 4.6.** Estimated Gross and Net Capital Stock of Singapore (S$ million in 2000 prices), 1960–2006.

| As at end Dec. | Gross capital stock | Net capital stock | As at end Dec. | Gross capital stock | Net capital stock |
|---|---|---|---|---|---|
| 1960 | 12,029 | 12,008 | 1984 | 179,016 | 130,766 |
| 1961 | 12,977 | 11,667 | 1985 | 195,735 | 142,179 |
| 1962 | 14,117 | 12,210 | 1986 | 209,079 | 150,466 |
| 1963 | 15,524 | 13,036 | 1987 | 221,977 | 158,204 |
| 1964 | 17,216 | 14,142 | 1988 | 234,983 | 166,194 |
| 1965 | 19,171 | 15,493 | 1989 | 249,914 | 176,121 |
| 1966 | 21,136 | 16,829 | 1990 | 267,304 | 187,243 |
| 1967 | 23,390 | 18,413 | 1991 | 287,442 | 200,437 |
| 1968 | 26,266 | 20,546 | 1992 | 310,387 | 215,678 |
| 1969 | 29,850 | 23,273 | 1993 | 335,254 | 232,697 |
| 1970 | 34,470 | 26,874 | 1994 | 362,228 | 251,578 |
| 1971 | 40,191 | 31,356 | 1995 | 392,167 | 273,437 |
| 1972 | 46,710 | 36,383 | 1996 | 430,502 | 302,681 |
| 1973 | 53,625 | 41,517 | 1997 | 473,147 | 334,975 |
| 1974 | 61,180 | 46,960 | 1998 | 513,543 | 362,673 |
| 1975 | 65,086 | 51,743 | 1999 | 551,199 | 386,707 |
| 1976 | 72,756 | 57,014 | 2000 | 590,344 | 412,351 |
| 1977 | 80,526 | 62,124 | 2001 | 630,914 | 435,491 |
| 1978 | 89,095 | 67,721 | 2002 | 665,165 | 451,938 |
| 1979 | 98,796 | 74,110 | 2003 | 696,585 | 465,782 |
| 1980 | 110,508 | 82,013 | 2004 | 729,716 | 482,333 |
| 1981 | 124,114 | 91,276 | 2005 | 761,277 | 497,634 |
| 1982 | 140,702 | 102,954 | 2006 | 797,035 | 516,521 |
| 1983 | 159,063 | 116,160 | | | |

*Source*: Writer's estimate using raw data from CEIC database.

depreciation. There are two different views on whether NCS or GCS is a better measure of productive capacity of a country. According to OECD (1993), GCS is more appropriate for measuring the contribution of capital assets to production, while net capital stock is more appropriate for measuring the wealth of asset holders. This view implicitly assumes that there is no decline in the productive efficiency of fixed assets due to aging, as wear and tear are made good through repair and maintenance until the assets reach the end of their service lives. However, if efficiency reduces as the assets age, which is highly likely for most assets groups, then NCS would be a better measure, as depreciation could serves as a surrogate for the reduced efficiency.

### 4.9. Appendix 2. Difficulties in the Measurement of Incremental Capital-Output Ratio

ICOR is defined as the amount of additional capital stock ($\Delta K$) needed to increase national output by one unit ($\Delta Y$). Since investment ($I$) measures the change in capital stock, ICOR is given by:

$$ICOR = \frac{\Delta K}{\Delta Y} = \frac{I_t}{Y_t - Y_{t-1}}.$$

ICOR is commonly computed by dividing "gross fixed capital formation" (GFCF) by changes in GDP. While seemingly easy to compute, it is very difficult to measure ICOR accurately, as the *theoretical* or *conceptual* ICOR can be quite different from the *measured* or *actual* ICOR, especially in the short term. Theoretical ICOR is the units of capital needed to increase output by one unit, while measured ICOR is the actual investment in fixed assets divided by the change in the GDP over the same period. Some of the factors that distort the level of ICOR include: the cyclical nature of national output, gestation period of projects, and the failure to account for depreciation.

The cyclical nature of economic output poses one of the biggest problems in the measurement of ICOR. One of the implicit assumptions for ICOR to be used as a measurement of marginal productivity of capital is that the economy is always operating at the "potential output" level. However, the actual level of GDP of a country is rarely at the level of "potential GDP". There are a variety of influences on GDP that are not attributable to changes in capital stock. Such examples are fluctuations in external demand, changes in fiscal and monetary policies and movements in resource prices. More often than not, changes in the level of ICOR are due to the fluctuations of output level, rather than changes in the efficiency of capital utilization. Many researchers have resorted to moving average approach, which averages the measured ICOR over a three-year, five-year, or even seven-year period to reduce the cyclical effect. However, if the output fluctuation is large, this method may still be unable to derive a truly representative mid-term ICOR.

The measurement of ICOR also implicitly assumes that that the increase in output in a year is due to the investment in the same year. Some researchers choose to lag investment by one year, which is to imply that the increase in output in a year is due to the investment in the previous year. However, many of the large-scale investment projects such as transport infrastructure and public works have long gestation periods that span over a few years. Thus, an increase in output this year could be due to an investment project that commenced many years ago but has only begun production this year. This would result in a higher measured ICOR in the preceding years, and a low measured ICOR this year.

Lastly, the ICOR is usually computed using gross investment, which does not take into account the depreciation of capital stock. In countries that are in the process of extensively renewing their capital stock, an example would be present-day China having to replace large amount of inferior capital stock created during its command-economy era, the net investment would be much lower than the gross investment. And thus, the ICOR would be overstated.

# CHAPTER 5

# The S-Curves of Singapore and Japan

## 5.1. Introduction

The miraculous economic development of Japan as it rose from the defeat of World War II and the phenomenal transformation of Singapore from a Third World development basket case in the early 1960s to a showcase state of present days have always been of interest to policy makers and academics. In the 1960s and 1970s, many developing economies looked up to Japan as a role model and attempted to emulate economic policies of Japan that they felt were responsible for the economic success of Japan. Controversial issues such as industrial targeting, Japan's Main Bank System and Japan's Iron Triangle have also been extensively debated. In the 1980s and 1990s, attentions were shifted to the newly industrializing economies (NIEs), which include Singapore, Hong Kong, South Korea and Taiwan. The success story of Singapore was of particular interest to the smaller developing countries, as Singapore has managed to rapidly ascend the development ladder despite its small size and lack of natural resources. The subsequent stagnation of Japan since the late 1980s has similarly attracted substantial interest from policy makers and academics.

In this chapter, the framework of the S-Curve hypothesis is applied to the case studies of Japan and Singapore to better our understanding of the economic transformation of these two countries. The application of the S-Curve hypothesis to the case study of Japan concludes that the S-Curve hypothesis is able to explain the rapid growth of the Japanese economy in the 1950s and 1960s and the eventual slowing down since the late 1980s. The case study also highlights an interesting observation that the transition process from a horse economy to an elephant economy is fairly long, and could stretch up to two decades. By comparing the macroeconomic indicators of Japan and Singapore, it is deduced that

Singapore is at the initial phase of a gradual transformation to an elephant economy. The real per capita GDP of Singapore is expected to grow at an average of 3.5% to 4% in the next 20 years and slow down to 1.5% to 2% thereafter.

The structure of this chapter is as follows: Sections 5.2 and 5.4 present the S-Curve of Singapore's and Japanese economies, and test for structural changes in these two economies using the Chow test. Sections 5.4 and 5.5 apply the S-Curve hypothesis to the case studies of Japan and Singapore. Section 5.6 concludes the chapter by discussing how Singapore could extend its growth potential and achieve higher growth level.

### 5.2. The S-Curve of Singapore's Economy

Figure 5.1 gives the log per capita income of Singapore over the last 45 years. The United States is included in the diagram for comparison. As explained in Chapter 1, the length of data series has to be sufficiently long

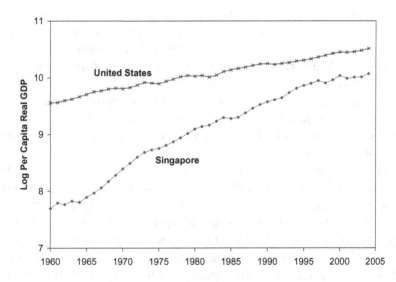

**Fig. 5.1.**   Log per capita real GDP (in US$) of Singapore and US, 1960–2004.

*Source*: Computed using data from WDI online (data extracted on 22 February 2006).

before the time plot of log per capita income of an economy is able to sketch out an S-Curve. This is because the time series has to contain two transition points: the economic take-off as the economy transforms from a turtle to a horse, and the eventual slow-down as it transforms from a horse to an elephant. Due to its very short development history, and the very rapid growth experienced during this period, Singapore's growth path was able to roughly sketch out the shape of an S-Curve even through the time series of only 45 years is very short.

The growth rate of Singapore's economy was visibly lower between 1960 and 1965 than the three decades thereafter. This indicates the transformation of Singapore's economy from a turtle to a horse economy. As the gap between the (log) per capita income level of the United States and that of Singapore narrowed, the growth momentum of Singapore appears to have slowed down in the last 10 years or so. In 2004, Singapore's per capita GDP was 65% of that of the United States. The combination of higher income levels and decelerating growth rates indicates that Singapore is gradually transforming into an elephant economy.

In order for a growth path to exhibit an S-Curve, there should be two structural changes, one occurring at the transformation from a turtle economy to a horse economy, and another occurring at the transformation from a horse economy to an elephant economy. The first structural change for Singapore is not tested due to the very short time series before 1965. We conduct the Chow test (Gujarati, 2003) for the second structural change at the point where Singapore's economy began its transformation from a horse to an elephant economy, which occurred around 1997.[1] Thus, the period that corresponds to the horse economy is 1965–1996, and the period that corresponds to the elephant economy is 1997–2004.

$$\text{Horse economy:} \quad Y_t = \alpha_1 + \alpha_2 t + \mu_{1t}, \quad t = 1, 2, \ldots, 32. \quad (1)$$

$$\text{Elephant economy:} \quad Y_t = \beta_1 + \beta_2 t + \mu_{2t}, \quad t = 1, 2, \ldots, 8. \quad (2)$$

---

[1] The S-Curve of economic development of an economy could also be fitted with a logistic model. However, due to the short data series before the first transition point, logistic model is not suitable for the Singapore's economy.

We first estimate $Y_t = \lambda_1 + \lambda_2 t + \mu_t$ for the full period from 1965 to 2004. The residual sum of squares (RSS), $S_1$, is 0.4754 with df = 38. Equations (1) and (2) are then estimated individually, and their respective RSS are $S_2 = 0.2060$ with df = 30 and $S_3 = 0.0060$ with df = 6. The sum of the two RSS is $S_4 = 0.2120$ with df = 36. We then obtain $S_5 = S_1 - S_4 = 0.2634$.

In this case, Chow test statistic $F = (S_5/2)/(S_4/36)$ follows the $F$ distribution with df = 2, 36. The computed $F = 22.36$ exceeds the critical $F$ value at 1% level. Thus we can reject significantly the hypothesis that the growth paths of the two periods are the same. In other words, there is a structural change in 1997, where Singapore's economy began its transformation into an elephant economy.

### 5.3. The S-Curve of Japan's Economy

Figure 5.2 shows the time path of the log per capita GDP of Japan from 1960 to 2004. It is evident from the figure that the time path underwent at least one structural change around 1974.

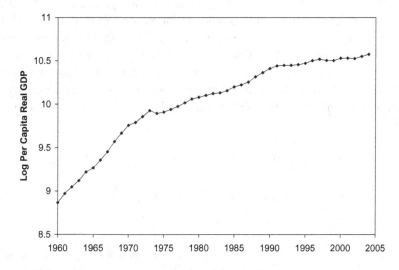

**Fig. 5.2.**   Log per capita real GDP (in US$) of Japan, 1960–2004.

*Source*: Computed using data from WDI online (data extracted on 22 February 2006).

The economic development of Japan has often been divided into two stages: pre-World War II and post-World War II. The first stage can be dated from the Meji Restoration in 1868 up to 1937 when Japan went to war with China. The war escalated to become World War II and it eventually ended in 1945 with the surrender of Japan and the occupation of Japan by the Allied Powers. Japan only regained its sovereignty in 1952. Thus, the second stage of Japan's economic development, which is also the focus of this chapter, refers to the period from 1952 till the present. In accordance with the S-Curve hypothesis and with the structural changes that were observed in Fig. 5.2, we further divide the second stage of the Japanese economic development into three phases as the 1950s–1960s (horse economy), the 1970s–1980s (gradual transition from horse to elephant economy), and the 1990s till the present (elephant economy).

We conduct the Chow test for the structural change at the point where the Japanese economy began its transformation from a horse to an elephant economy. Visual inspection indicates that the structural change occurred in 1974. Thus, the period that corresponds to the horse economy is 1960–1974, and the period that corresponds to the elephant economy is 1975–2004.

$$\text{Horse economy:} \quad Y_t = \alpha_1 + \alpha_2 t + \mu_{1t} \quad t = 1, 2,..., 15. \quad (3)$$

$$\text{Elephant economy:} \quad Y_t = \beta_1 + \beta_2 t + \mu_{2t} \quad t = 1, 2,..., 30. \quad (4)$$

$Y_t = \lambda_1 + \lambda_2 t + \mu_t$ is first estimated for the full period from 1960 to 2004. The residual sum of squares (RSS), $S_1$, is obtained as 0.8428 with df = 43. Equations (3) and (4) are then estimated individually, and their respective RSS are $S_2 = 0.0238$ with df = 13 and $S_3 = 0.0658$ with df = 28. The sum of the two RSS is $S_4 = 0.0896$ with df = 41. We then obtain $S_5 = S_1 - S_4 = 0.7532$.

The Chow test statistic $F = (S_5/2)/(S_4/41)$ follows the $F$ distribution with df = 2, 41. The computed $F = 172.28$ exceeds the critical $F$ value at 1% level. Thus the growth paths of the two periods are significantly different, and we can conclude that the Japanese economy underwent a structural change in 1974.

## 5.4.  Economic Transformation of Japan from Horse to Elephant Economy

The Japanese economy provides an interesting case study in illustrating the S-Curve hypothesis as it represents a horse economy that has transformed into an elephant economy in the last two to three decades.

Figure 5.3 shows the time trends of the various economic indicators of Japan as it underwent economic transformation. The diagrams throw

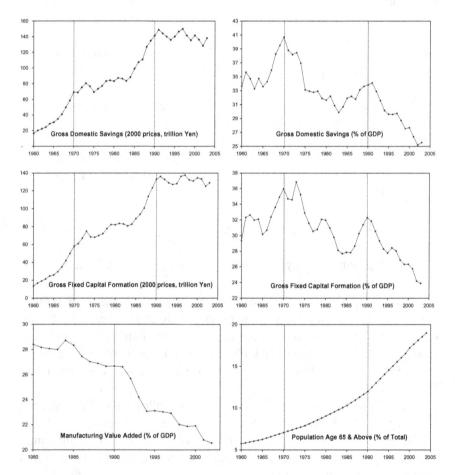

**Fig. 5.3.**  Transformation of the Japanese economy from horse economy to elephant economy.

*Source*: Computed from data from WDI online (data extracted on 14 February 2006).

**Table 5.1.** Characteristics of the Japanese economy in various phases of development.

| | Horse | Horse → Elephant | Elephant |
|---|---|---|---|
| Gross domestic savings | ↑ | ↑ | Plateau |
| Gross domestic savings (% GDP) | ↑ (34% in 1960) | ↓ (32% in 1980) | ↓ (28% in 2000) |
| Gross fixed capital formation | ↑ | ↑ | Plateau |
| Gross fixed capital formation (% GDP) | ↑ (29% in 1960) | ↓ (32% in 1980) | ↓ (24% in 2000) |
| Manufacturing value added (% GDP) | n.a. | ↓ (28% in 1980) | ↓ (22% in 2000) |
| Aged (% of total population) | ↑ (6% in 1960) | ↑ (9% in 1980) | ↑ (17% in 2000) |

*Note*: ↑ denotes increasing, ↓ denotes decreasing.
*Source*: Computed from data from WDI online (data extracted on 14 February 2006).

light on the structural changes of the economy as it transformed from a horse economy to an elephant economy. Based on information available in Fig. 5.3, Table 5.1 provides a summary of economic indicators of Japan during its various phases of development.

Comparing the trends of the economic indicators given in Table 5.1, it can be seen that gross domestic savings (GDS) as a percentage of GDP and gross fixed capital formation (GFCF) as a percentage of GDP reversed their upward trend as Japan transformed from a horse to an elephant economy. Furthermore, GDS in absolute value and GFCF in absolute value reached a plateau as Japan became a matured elephant economy.

### 5.4.1. *Galloping horse: the 1950s–1960s*

After World War II had ended, Japan was devastated. The industries and the transportation networks in most of the large cities were severely damaged. Japan was also plagued by a severe shortage of food for several years. However, in the following 20 years, Japan miraculously rose from the ruins and defeat of World War II. Using data from the Penn World

Table 6.1 that was PPP-adjusted, Japan's per capita GDP grew at a superlative average annual rate of 7.7% between 1952 and 1973. The comparative growth rate of the US economy over the same period was only 2.4%. At the end of the Allied Occupation, Japan was a "less-developed" country, but over the next twenty years, Japan was able to become the first "less-developed" country in the postwar era to achieve the "developed" status.

According to the S-Curve hypothesis, rapid capital accumulation and technology transfer are the key drivers behind high growth rates of the horse economies. It can be seen from Fig. 5.3 that Japan's savings and investment rates were on the upward climb and peaked at the end of this period. Furthermore, non-residential capital stock per worker grew at an impressive 12.9% per annum[2] between 1965 and 1973. At the same time, Japan improved its technological capability through technology licensing, patent purchases, and imitation and improvement of foreign inventions. Other factors such as Japan's industrious and well-educated workforce, excellent management and labor relations, government industrial policies, and conducive political and international environment also contributed to the rapid economic development of Japan (Lim, 1991).

### 5.4.2. *Gradual transformation into an elephant economy: the 1970s–1980s*

The Japanese economy slowed down significantly during the 1970s and 1980s with the average annual growth rate of its PPP-adjusted per capita GDP decelerated to 3.4%. However, the growth rate still compared very favorably to the 2.4% growth rate experienced by the United States over the same period.

The slowdown was triggered by the oil crisis in 1973. Higher oil price was sometimes cited as the reason behind the slower growth rate of the Japanese economy since then. However, Japan adjusted and overcame the higher oil prices via the adoption and production of fuel-efficient machineries. The persistent lower growth rates in the two decades after the oil crisis can be better explained by the rapidly diminishing opportunities of quantum-leap in technology transfer. As the Japanese level of

---

[2] Computed from data from PWT 5.6 (Heston *et al.*, 1995).

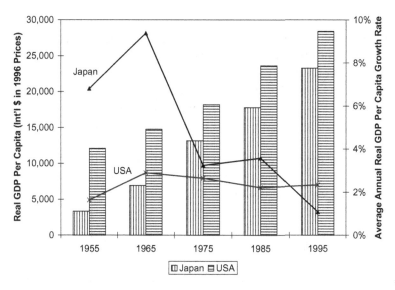

**Fig. 5.4.** Comparison between Japan's and US's real GDP per capita (PPP-adjusted) and real GDP per capita growth rates, the 1950s–1990s.

*Note*: Real GDP growth rates refer to the average annual growth rates in the 1950s, 1960s, 1970s, 1980s and 1990s.

*Source*: Computed from data from PWT 6.1 (Heston *et al.*, 2002).

economic development and technological know-how was catching up fast with the other developed nations, Japan can no longer easily borrow and imitate technological innovations from other developed countries at relatively low cost. Japan has to invest heavily in R&D in order to forge ahead of the pack of developed nations. Figure 5.4 shows the catching up of the Japanese economy with the US economy. In 1955, Japan's PPP-adjusted per capita GDP was only a quarter of that of the United States. This ratio rose steadily to 47% in 1965, 72% in 1975, 75% in 1985 and more than 80% in 1995. In terms of ranking of per capita GDP, Japan ranked 5th in 1990, only behind Luxembourg, the United States, Switzerland and Canada. It can also be seen from Fig. 5.4 that as the gap between the per capita income levels of the two countries narrowed, so has the gap between their growth rates. Using the terminology of the S-Curve hypothesis, Japan was approaching the tail-end of the horse phase of the S-Curve during the 1970s and 1980s, and thus growth rates were slowing down to a level that is comparable to those of the developed nations.

The structure of the Japanese economy was also gradually transforming during this period. It can be seen from Fig. 5.3 that the savings and investment rates reversed their upward climb from about 1970 and started their descend, although in terms of absolute values, gross domestic savings and gross fixed capital formation were still increasing. At the same time, the contribution of the manufacturing sector was gradually diminishing while the percentage of aged in the population was slowly increasing.

It is interesting to note that the transformation of the Japanese economy from a horse economy to an elephant economy was very gradual; it spanned across a period of almost 20 years.

### 5.4.3. *Matured elephant economy: the 1990s–present*

The Japanese per capita GDP further slowed down to 1.1% during the 1990s. This slowdown has often been attributed to the signing of the Plaza Accord in 1985 and the subsequent busting of the asset price bubble in Japan in the late 1980s. According to the Plaza Accord, the then G-5 nations (France, West Germany, Japan, the United States and the United Kingdom) agreed to devalue the US dollar in relation to the Japanese Yen and German Deutsche Mark by intervening in currency markets. The exchange rate value of the Dollar versus the Yen declined by 50% over the two years after the agreement took place, and continued to slide after the end of the coordinated interventions due to currency speculation. The intended result of the Plaza Accord was never achieved as the trade deficit of the United States with Japan was not alleviated. McKinnon (2005) argues that the currency depreciation by Japan slowed the economic growth of the Japanese economy and eventually caused deflation.

However, the appreciation of the Japanese Yen cannot fully explain the persistently low rates of growth of Japan since 1990, a period that spanned more than a decade. Japan adopted the floating exchange rate system in 1973, after 24 years of pegging the Japanese Yen to the US Dollar. Since then, the overall trend of the exchange rate of the Japanese Yen from 1973 to 2004 was that of a gradual appreciation (see Fig. 5.5). In other words, the appreciation of the Japanese Yen against the US Dollar was not a sudden event in 1985, but has started taking place as early as 1973. Furthermore, Lim (1991) notes that "despite the remarkable appreciation of the Yen in the 1970s and 1980s, the Japanese export competitiveness

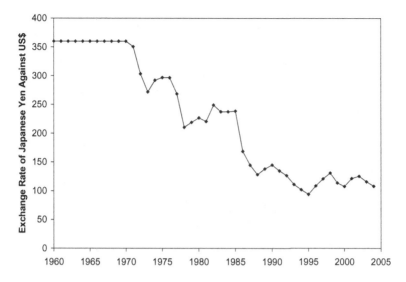

**Fig. 5.5.** Exchange rate of Japanese Yen against US Dollar, 1960–2004.

*Note*: Exchange rates based on period average.

*Source*: Computed from data from WDI online (data extracted on 30 March 2006).

has not appeared to have declined." An appreciation of the Japanese Yen, albeit coerced, does not necessarily imply that the Japanese Yen is overvalued. The current account of Japan has been uninterruptedly recording surpluses since 1981; post-1985 current account surpluses remained substantial, averaging 2.7% of GDP between 1986 and 2004 (see Fig. 5.6). In addition, Japan has been steadily accumulating foreign reserves, with a quickening of pace post-1985. Its foreign reserves reached US$847 billion in 2005, which was the highest in the world (see Fig. 5.7). All these suggest that the appreciation of the Japanese Yen had not hurt the export competitiveness of Japan, and thus cannot be the chief reason behind the slow growth rate of Japan.

The slowing down of the Japanese economy has more to do with the intrinsic characteristics of an elephant economy than with its currency appreciation. Against the framework of the S-Curve hypothesis, the slowing down of the Japanese economy is a totally-expectable outcome. Elephant economies simply do not grow rapidly. There is no theoretical or empirical support that a matured economy can grow at a superlative rate.

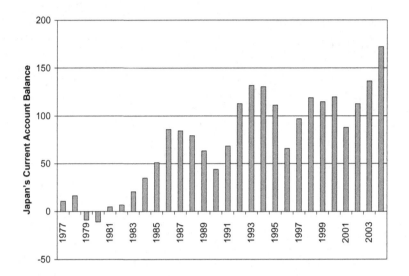

**Fig. 5.6.**    Japan's current account balance (in billion US$), 1977–2004.

*Source*: Computed from data from WDI online (data extracted on 30 March 2006).

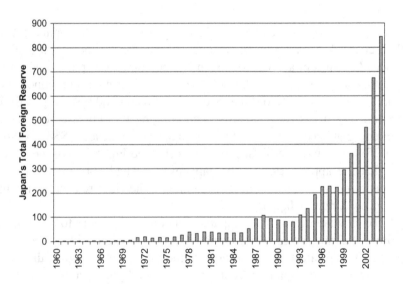

**Fig. 5.7.**    Japan's total foreign reserve (in billion US$), 1960–2004.

*Source*: Computed from data from WDI online (data extracted on 16 February 2006).

As its economy matured, Japan, like many other elephant economies, was facing falling savings and investment rates. Figure 5.3 shows that in terms of absolute values, Japan's gross domestic savings and gross fixed capital formation reached a plateau in 1990s after several decades of rapid growth, while its savings and investment rates continued with the decline that had started since early 1970s. And like many other elephant economies, Japan is experiencing de-industrialization and aging population. Figure 5.3 shows the steady decline of Japan's manufacturing value added as a percentage of GDP from 28% during the early 1980s to 20% in 2002. The high wage cost and land cost in Japan are spurring the relocation of its manufacturing activities to cheaper and less developed countries. At the same time, Japan is also facing a rapidly aging population which saw the percentage of population aged 65 and above increase from less than 6% in 1960 to almost 20% in 2004. As described in Chapter 1, all these factors will lead to a substantial slowdown in the growth rate of the Japanese economy.

## 5.5. Is Singapore an Elephant Economy?

If the application of the S-Curve hypothesis to the Japanese economy could be considered a post-mortem analysis which provides a case study for referencing, the application of the S-Curve hypothesis to Singapore's economy would provide a tool to project the future performance of Singapore's economy. In particular, it would be interesting to ascertain if Singapore has begun its transformation into an elephant economy, and how long it would take before Singapore becomes a matured elephant economy that is destined to have a low rate of GDP growth.

The log per capita real GDP of Singapore in Fig. 5.1 shows that Singapore's economy started to take off around 1965. That could be taken as the turning point when Singapore transformed from a slow-growing turtle economy into a fast-growing horse economy. What is less obvious is whether the seemingly tapering off of Singapore's log per capita real GDP from 2000 onwards signals the gradual transformation of Singapore from a horse economy to an elephant economy. And if it is so, how long would it take before Singapore fully transforms into an elephant economy and thereby entering a long-term phase of slow growth.

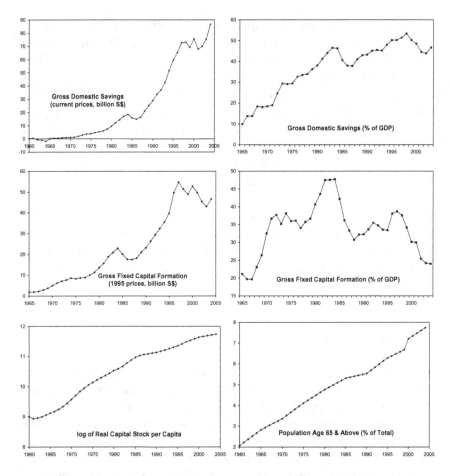

**Fig. 5.8.**   Transformation of Singapore's economy.

*Source*: Computed from data from WDI online (data extracted on 16 February 2006). Data on real capital stock per capita are estimated by writer using raw data from CEIC database (see Chapter 6 for more details).

Figure 5.8 shows the time trends of the various economic indicators of Singapore in the last four decades. Comparison with the experiences of Japan (see Fig. 5.3) highlights some interesting similarities and differences. In terms of absolute values, Japanese gross domestic savings was steadily increasing up till the early 1990s when it reached a plateau. However, as a percentage of GDP, Japanese savings rate was on its decline since the early 1970s and has fallen to almost 25% in 2004. On the other hand, although Singapore's savings rate has halted its unrelenting upward climb since 1985, it was able to hold up at a level of more than 40% in the last 15 years or so. Thus, in terms of savings rates, Singapore has yet to show signs of transformation into an elephant economy.

However, data on gross fixed capital formation (GFCF) appears to indicate that Singapore has begun its transformation into an elephant economy. The value of GFCF reversed its upward trend in 1998 during the Asian Financial Crisis. If this post-1997 period is taken to correspond to the post-1990 period in Japan, this would indicate that Singapore has already become an elephant economy. The picture painted by the GFCF as a percentage of GDP also presents similar conclusions. GFCF in terms of percentage of GDP began its downward slide in 1985, with the value halving from 48% in 1984 to 24% in 2004. In comparison, Japan's gross fixed capital formation was also 24% of GDP in 2003.

The conflicting conclusions presented by the savings and investment rates of the two countries can in part be attributed to the differences in the macroeconomic management by the governments of these two countries. Japanese government has undertaken large-scale pump-priming projects in the 1990s in an attempt to counter the recessionary gap in the country; this in turn drove down domestic savings. Thus, as compared to an economy at a similar stage of development but did not undertake as many pump priming projects, Japan would have a higher investment rate but a lower savings rate.

In terms of population profile, Singapore experiences ageing population too, with the percentage of aged steadily increasing from 2.1% in 1960 to 7.7% in 2004. In comparison, the corresponding figure of Japan was 7.1% in 1970, the initial year of the gradual transformation of the Japanese economy to an elephant economy.

The comparison with the economic indicators of Japan suggests that Singapore is likely to be in between a galloping horse and a matured elephant. It is at the initial phase of gradual transformation to an elephant economy. And using the experience of Japan as a guide, real per capita GDP of Singapore is projected to grow at an average rate of 3.5% to 4% in the next twenty years. Thereafter, average long-term annual growth rate is expected to slow down to 1.5% to 2%.

## 5.6. Conclusion: Pushing the Envelope of Growth Potential of Singapore

Using the experience of Japan as a guide, Singapore is predicted to become a matured elephant economy in around 20 years time, growing at an estimated average annual growth rate of about 3.6%.[3] Of course Singapore might not and need not follow the development path of Japan. As explained in Chapter 1, each country has its own unique S-Curve, and there would be a range of per capita GDP levels among the matured elephant economies. While it is inevitable that Singapore has already embarked on the journey of a gradual transformation from a horse economy to an elephant economy, Singapore could try to remain on the growth path of 3.5% to 4% for a period of more than 20 years, or to grow at a rate that is higher than 3.5% to 4%. What can Singapore do to achieve that?

The S-Curve hypothesis tells us that the high rate of growth enjoyed by the horse economies is due to the high rate of fixed capital investment and quantum-leap in technological capability due to technology transfer. After accumulating substantial level of fixed capital stock, Singapore faces diminishing returns from additional fixed capital investment. It is unwise to single-mindedly pursuing a high rate of fixed capital investment when the marginal benefits do not match the marginal costs. Going forward, the rate of fixed capital investment is likely to fall further. At the same time, as the gap of technological capability in Singapore and that of the other developed nations narrows, Singapore can no longer easily reap the quantum-leap in technological improvements from technology transfer. Singapore has to increasingly rely on indigenous innovation for growth. In this aspect, the Singapore government's efforts in grooming our local talents through the A*STAR program[4] is a far-sighted strategy, and if executed properly to allow for sufficient downward linkages to the manufacturing sector, would enable Singapore to grow at a higher rate over a longer period of time.

---

[3] The 3.6% is computed from the per capita GDP growth rate of Japan between 1970 and 1989. It is taken as the estimated growth rate of a transiting elephant economy.

[4] A*STAR stands for Agency for Science, Technology and Research. The agency promotes, supports and oversees the public sector R&D research activities in Singapore and nurtures scientific talents through scholarships.

# Bibliography

Acemoglu, D and F Zilibotti (1997). Was Prometheus Unbound by Chance? Risk, Diversification, and Growth. *Journal of Political Economy*, 105(4), 709–751.

Aghion, P and P Howitt (1992). A Model of Growth Through Creative Destruction. *Econometrica*, 60(2), 323–351.

Andersson, L (2001). Openness and Total Factor Productivity in Swedish Manufacturing, 1980–1995. *Review of World Economics*, 137(4), 690–713.

Barro, RJ (1991). Economic Growth in a Cross-section of Countries. *Quarterly Journal of Economics*, 106(2), 407–444.

Barro, RJ and X Sala-i-Martin (1995). *Economic Growth*. McGraw-Hill, Singapore.

Barro, RJ and X Sala-i-Martin (1997). Technological Diffusion, Convergence, and Growth. *Journal of Economic Growth*, 2(1), 1–26.

Blomstrom, M, RE Lipsey and M Zejan (1996). Is Fixed Investment the Key to Economic Growth? *Quarterly Journal of Economics*, 111(1), 269–276.

Bosworth, BP and SM Collins (2003). The Empirics of Growth: An Update. *Brookings Papers on Economic Activity*, 2003(2), 113–206.

Bregman, A and A Marom (1999). Productivity Factors in Israel's Manufacturing Industry, 1960–1996. *Bank of Israel's Economic Review*, 72, 51–75.

Cook, P and C Kirkpatrick (1997). Globalization, Regionalization and Third World Development. *Regional Studies*, 31(1), 55–66.

Cunado, J, LA Gil-Alana and F Perez de Gracia (2004). Real Convergence in Taiwan: A Fractionally Integrated Approach. *Journal of Asian Economics*, 15(3), 529–547.

De Long, JB and LH Summers (1991). Equipment Investment and Economic Growth. *Quarterly Journal of Economics*, 106(2), 445–502.

De Long, JB and LH Summers (1992). Equipment Investment and Economic Growth: How Strong is the Nexus? *Brookings Papers on Economic Activity*, 1992(2), 157–199.

De Long, JB and LH Summers (1993). How Strongly Do Developing Economies Benefit from Equipment Investment? *Journal of Monetary Economics*, 32(3), 395–415.

Department of Statistics (1997). *Multifactor Productivity Growth in Singapore: Concept, Methodology and Trends*. Department of Statistics, Singapore.

Durlauf, SN and DT Quah (1999). The New Empirics of Economic Growth. In J Taylor and M Woodford (eds.), *Handbook of Macroeconomics* (Vol. 1A). North-Holland, Elsevier Science, Amsterdam and New York.

Easterly, W, M Kremer, L Pritchett and LH Summers (1993). Good Policy or Good Luck? Country Growth Performance and Temporary Shocks. *Journal of Monetary Economics*, 32(3), 459–483.

Easterly, W and R Levine (1997). Africa's Growth Tragedy: Policies and Ethnic Divisions. *Quarterly Journal of Economics*, 112(4), 1203–1250.

Easterly, W and R Levine (2001). What Have We Learned From a Decade of Empirical Research on Growth? It's Not Factor Accumulation: Stylized Facts and Growth Models. *World Bank Economic Review*, 15(2), 177–219.

Eggertsson, G (2004). Medium-Term Growth Prospects. In *Singapore: Selected Issues*. International Monetary Fund, Washington.

Fukuyama, F (2004). *State-Building: Governance and World Order in the Twenty-First Century*. Profile Books Ltd, London.

Ghali, KH and A Al-Mutawa (1999). The Intertemporal Causal Dynamics between Fixed Capital Formation and Economic Growth in the Group-of-Seven Countries. *International Economic Journal*, 13(2), 31–37.

Ghesquiere, H (2006). *Singapore's Success: Engineering Economic Growth*. Thomson Learning Asia, Singapore.

Gianaris, NV (1970). International Differences in Capital-Output Ratios. *American Economic Review*, 60(3), 465–477.

Grossman, GM and E Helpman (1991). Endogenous Product Cycles. *Economic Journal*, 101(408), 1214–1229.

Gujarati, DN (2003). Basic Econometrics, 4th ed. McGraw-Hill, Boston.

Hall, RE and CI Jones (1999). Why Do Some Countries Produce So Much More Output Per Worker Than Others? *Quarterly Journal of Economics*, 114(1), 83–116.

Hatemi-J, A and M Irandoust (2002). Investigating Causal Relations between Fixed Investment and Economic Growth. *Economia Internazionale/International Economics*, 55(1), 25–35.

Heston, A, R Summers and B Aten (2002). *Penn World Table Version 6.1*. Center for International Comparisons at the University of Pennsylvania (CICUP).

Heston, A, R Summers, DA Nuxoll and B Aten (1995). *Penn World Table Version 5.6*. Center for International Comparisons at the University of Pennsylvania (CICUP).

Hill, H and S Hill (2005). Growth Econometrics in the Tropics: What Insights for Southeast Asian Economic Development? *Singapore Economic Review*, 50, 313–343.

Hsiao, F and M-CW Hsiao (2004). Catching Up and Convergence: Long-run Growth in East Asia. *Review of Development Economics*, 8(2), 223–236.

Hsieh, CT (2002). What Explains the Industrial Revolution in East Asia? Evidence From Factor Markets. *American Economic Review*, 92(3), 502–526.

Huang, Y (2005). *From Moscow to Beijing and Places in Between: Personal Reflections of a World Bank Country Director.* Paper presented at the IPS Corporate Associates Appreciation Dinner.

Hulten, CR and FC Wykoff (1981). The Measurement of Economic Depreciation. In CR Hulten (ed.), *Depreciation, Inflation, and the Taxation of Income from Capital*. The Urban Institute Press, Washington, D.C.

Jun, Z (2003). Investment, Investment Efficiency, and Economic Growth in China. *Journal of Asian Economics*, 14(5), 713–734.

Kaufmann, D, A Kraay and M Mastruzzi (2006). *Governance Matters V: Aggregate and Individual Governance Indicators for 1996–2005*. The World Bank, Washington, D.C.

King, R and R Levine (1994). Capital Fundamentalism, Economic Development, and Economic Growth. *Carnegie-Rochester Conference Series on Public Policy*, 40, 259–292.

Kirkpatrick, C (1994). Institutional Capacity, Political Commitment and Export Assistance in Developing Countries. *Journal of International Development*, 6(5), 519–528.

Koh, SW, S Rahman and GKR Tan (2002). Growth and Productivity in Singapore Manufacturing Industries: 1975–1998. *Asian Economic Journal*, 16(3), 247–266.

Krugman, P (1994). The Myth of Asia's Miracle. *Foreign Affairs,* 73, 62–78.

Lim, CY (1984). The Causes of Development. *Singapore Economic Review,* 29(2), 63–82.

Lim, CY (1991). *Development and Underdevelopment*. Longman, Singapore.

Lim, CY (1994). Which Nations Will Dominate the World? A Review Article on Lester Thurow's Head to Head. *Accounting and Business Review*, 1(2), 261–273.

Lim, CY (1996). The Trinity Growth Theory: The Ascendancy of Asia and the Decline of the West. *Accounting and Business Review*, 3(2), 175–199.

Lim, CY (1997). The Low-Income Trap: Theory and Evidence. *Accounting and Business Review*, 4(1), 1–19.

Lim, CY (2005). *Economic Theory and the East Asian Region*. Paper presented at the Singapore Economic Review Conference, Singapore.

Lim, CY (2009). *Southeast Asia: The Long Road Ahead*, 3rd ed. World Scientific Publishing, Singapore.

Lucas, REJ (2002). *Lectures on Economic Growth*. Harvard University Press, Cambridge, Massachusetts.

Lucas, REJ (2004). The Industrial Revolution: Past and Future. *The Region,* Federal Reserve Bank of Minneapolis, 2004 (May), pp. 5–20.

Mauro, P (1995). Corruption and Growth. *Quarterly Journal of Economics,* 110(3), 681–712.

McKinnon, R (2005). *Exchange Rate or Wage Changes in International Adjustment? Japan and China versus the United States.* Paper presented at the Singapore Economic Review Conference, Singapore.

Nehru, V and A Dhareshwar (1993). A New Database on Physical Capital Stock: Sources, Methodology and Results. *Rivista de Analisis Economico,* 8(1), 37–59.

Ng, YK and X Yang (1999). Specialization, Information, and Growth: A Sequential Equilibrium Analysis. Center for International Development at Harvard University, CID Working Papers.

OECD (1993). *Methods Used by OECD Countries to Measure Stocks of Fixed Capital.* OECD, Paris.

OECD (2001). *Measuring Capital: A Manual on the Measurement of Capital Stocks, Consumption of Fixed Capital and Capital Services.* OECD, Paris.

Olson, M (1993). Dictatorship, Democracy, and Development. *American Political Science Reivew,* 87(3), 567–576.

Phillips, PCB and D Sul (2003). The Elusive Empirical Shadow of Growth Convergence. Cowles Foundation, Yale University, Cowles Foundation Discussion Paper No. 1398.

Phillips, PCB and D Sul (2005). Economic Transition and Growth. Cowles Foundation, Yale University, Cowles Foundation Discussion Paper No. 1514.

Podrecca, E and G Carmeci (2001). Fixed Investment and Economic Growth: New Results of Causality. *Applied Economics,* 33(2), 177–182.

Quah, D (1993). Empirical Cross-Section Dynamics in Economic Growth. *European Economic Review,* 37(2–3), 426–434.

Rao, VVB and C Lee (1995). Sources of Growth in the Singapore Economy and its Manufacturing and Service Sectors. *Singapore Economic Review,* 1(40), 83–115.

Rivera-Batiz, LA and PM Romer (1991). Economic Integration and Endogenous Growth. *Quarterly Journal of Economics,* 106(2), 531–555.

Romer, PM (1990). Endogenous Technological Change. *Journal of Political Economy,* 98(5), 71–102.

Sarel, M (1997). Growth and Productivity in ASEAN Countries, IMF Working Paper No. 97/97. Washington, D.C.: International Monetary Fund.

Sng HY, S Rahman and WM Chia (2009). Economic Growth and Transition: A Stochastic Technological Diffusion Model. *Journal of Economic Development,* 34(2), 1–25.

Solow, RM (1956). A Contribution to the Theory of Economic Growth. *Quarterly Journal of Economics,* 70(1), 65–94.

Temple, JR and PA Johnson (1998). Social Capability and Economic Growth. *Quarterly Journal of Economics*, 113(3), 965–990.

Tsao, Y (1982). *Growth and Productivity in Singapore: A Supply Side Analysis.* Unpublished PhD Thesis, Harvard University.

Wu, F and JP Thia (2002). Total Factor Productivity with Singaporean Characteristics: Adjusting for Impact of Housing Investment and Foreign Workers. In *Economic Survey of Singapore*. Ministry of Trade and Industry, Singapore.

Young, A (1992). A Tale of Two Cities: Factor Accumulation and Technical Change in Hong Kong and Singapore. In OJ Blanchard and S Fischer (eds.), *NBER Macroeconomics Annual 1992*. MIT Press, Cambridge, MA.

Young, A (1995). The Tyranny of Numbers: Confronting the Statistical Realities of the East Asian Growth Experience. *Quarterly Journal of Economics*, 110, 641–680.

# Index